LEAD NOW!

A Personal Leadership
Coaching Guide
For Results-Driven Leaders

John Parker Stewart
and
Daniel J. Stewart

1st Edition Printed 2009
under the title *The Development Advisor*

J.P. Stewart Systems, Inc
PO Box 1527, Lake Oswego, OR 97035
503.638.1106
www.johnparkerstewart.com

Published by Leadership Excellence
www.LeaderExcel.com

Library of Congress Cataloging-in-Publication Data

ISBN: 978-1-930771-40-6

Printed in the United States of America

Also by John Parker Stewart:

52 Leadership Gems: Practical and Quick Insights for Leading Others

52 Leadership Lessons: Timeless Stories for the Modern Leader

Winning Orals: The Master Formula for Securing Government Contracts

Advance Praise

"The single most important asset that drives a successful business is the strength of its leadership. *LEAD NOW!* provides an action-oriented change management plan for improving your leadership skills. Implementation of this book will result in improved strategic planning, program performance, customer satisfaction and personal development. John and Daniel capture and apply their decades of experience in coaching and organizational development in a book that provides a 'can do' method to evolve your leadership skills. I endorse this book and believe it is one that every leader should use for practical application of leadership techniques."

Carey A. Smith, President,
Honeywell Technology Solutions Inc.

"John Parker Stewart is without a doubt one of the most profound, inspirational, and passionate executive coaches in business training. His coaching tips cover all crucial points that you need to know in leading an organization. John makes the complex simple and the difficult do-able. It will be the best training in your career!"

Jiangong R. Dai, CEO,
Soufun Holdings Ltd., Beijing, China

"Thank Goodness John Parker Stewart has finally put these coaching tips into print! Now I can get rid of all the crib notes I have jotted down from conversations with him as I faced new or rapidly changing leadership challenges. This isn't another management book. It is a compilation of the right things John has observed leaders do over the thirty plus years he has worked with leaders and leadership development. I wouldn't go into bear country without a gun. I certainly won't go into the boardroom without *LEAD NOW!* Thank you, John!"

Ken Asbury, former President,
Lockheed Martin Technical Operations
current President and CEO, ASRC FEDERAL

"For years, John Parker Stewart has been propelling the 'Top Talent' inside major companies to new levels of leadership. The art of great leadership requires excellent listening, thoughtful analysis, great communication and quick actions combined with flexibility. In *LEAD NOW!* JPS brings it all together in a practical, easy to access, actionable package that is a must read for anyone who wants to be a better leader."

Will Irving, former General Counsel
and Current Group Managing Director,
Telstra Business of Telstra,
Sydney and Melbourne Australia

"*LEAD NOW!* is an easy to use leadership reference guide full of time-tested insights, practical 'how-to' advice and easy to use tools that allow readers to quickly build personalized action plans for sustained change. It will become an indispensable handbook for both those new to leadership and seasoned veterans alike."

Michael Millane, Principal Program Manager, Intel Corp

"I highly recommend *LEAD NOW!* John Parker Stewart is the best I have encountered to lead an organization through the process of improving the skills of its leaders. His techniques work! My teams and I have benefitted from his guidance many times over the past 15 years. Grasp his coaching tips in *LEAD NOW!* and you will be a better person, and a better leader. I use them every day."

Jay F Honeycutt, former Center Director (CEO),
Kennedy Space Center
Former President,
Lockheed Martin Space Operations

"John Parker Stewart has produced a must have reference book for all aspiring leaders. *LEAD NOW!* is the 'go to' guide for others that claim to already be leaders. Successful companies are where each senior manager is both an integral part of a team of leaders and the leader of a team—this book can be the handbook to achieve this!"

Ray Kiley, BSc/LLB(Hons), Chief Operating Officer,
Medibank Health Solutions,
New Zealand & Australia

"I fully endorse *LEAD NOW!* I have greatly benefited from John's insightful and practical leadership teachings.

His vast experience, positive energy and passion for developing leaders at all levels create common sense concepts and solutions that can directly and easily be applied to both personal and professional leadership challenges."

Michael A Dignam, President and CEO, PAE

Dedication

To the thousands of leaders we have coached over the past decades. You have come to us from every country and every industry with challenges that cover the spectrum of managerial life. Your desire to learn, progress and succeed has been a driving force in our lives. To you, we salute you and dedicate this book!

Contents

Contrary to the opinion of many people, leaders are NOT born. Leaders are made, and they are made by effort and hard work.

—Vince Lombardi

Introduction

This book came about as a result of our years of observing extremely busy leaders. Most leaders want to improve, but can barely find the time to manage all that they are already doing. Our motivation in seeking the *LEAD NOW!* concept was to develop a model that is practical, useful, easy to teach, easy to understand, and smacks of common sense! We have included in this book the *LEAD NOW!* model (see next page), coaching tips under each of our 21 leadership dimensions, exercises for your own effectiveness and your team's effectiveness, and an action planning section. You will find a practical list of personalized coaching steps toward your individual progress in becoming a great leader.

The *LEAD NOW!* Leadership Development Model was created to provide leaders at all levels a simple and comprehensive framework for the critical areas of leading others. The model is based on over 50 years of collective management and leadership consulting and coaching experience with Fortune 500 companies, government organizations, and start-ups. Combining this professional experience with industry best practices and academic research, the *LEAD NOW!* Model offers a solid foundation for busy leaders to build and refine their skills as they practice the art of being a leader in today's changing environment.

LEAD NOW! MODEL

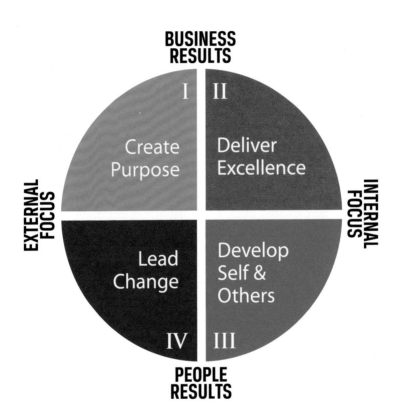

BUSINESS
RESULTS

I — Create Purpose

II — Deliver Excellence

EXTERNAL FOCUS

INTERNAL FOCUS

IV — Lead Change

III — Develop Self & Others

PEOPLE
RESULTS

This model is built on the assumption that leaders must achieve aligned and positive results from four perspectives: 1) their people, 2) their business, 3) their marketplace (external), and 4) their organization (internal). These four points of view become the two axes that encompass the four areas of great leadership: *Create*

Purpose, Deliver Excellence, Develop Self & Others, and *Lead Change*. Each of these four quadrants is supported by 4-7 key leadership dimensions and provides the basis for in-depth leadership development action planning.

Leadership is critical to an organization's performance and leaders become better through focused and supported development. The *LEAD NOW!* Leadership Development Model provides the foundation for any personalized leadership development effort, whether it is a coaching engagement, a workshop, or a larger leadership program.

Using the *LEAD NOW!* model will help you identify and improve the behaviors needed to increase your success in leading others and achieving desired organizational results.

The bulk of this book consists of hundreds of practical coaching tips and resources organized by *21 Leadership Dimensions*. These quotes, tips, and book resources are designed for your busy life. They are organized into the four quadrants of the model. At the end of each Dimension you will find a self-assessment section that contains key questions to help you reflect on your current leadership skills and attitudes. This is followed by an action planning section to enable you to set specific goals for improvement.

LEAD NOW! MODEL
21 Leadership Dimensions

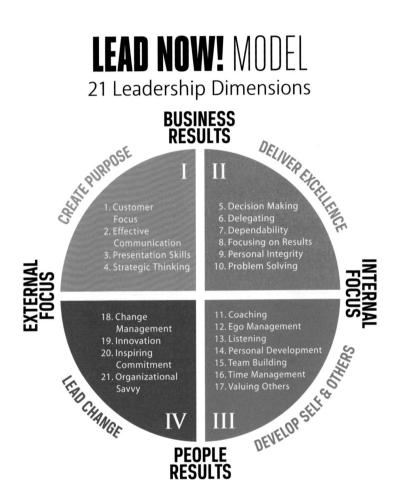

At the end of the book, you will find additional leadership exercises. These are designed to be helpful guides whether you are moving to a new leadership role at work, working with a new staff, or simply seeking improvement in your current position.

Throughout *LEAD NOW!* you will see the following icons. They are meant as a guide to help you use this handbook more effectively. This is what they mean:

The businessperson icon represents opportunities for self-assessment. These sections will allow you to critically analyze your own leadership capacities, skills, and behaviors.

The pencil icon indicates "notes" sections—pages provided for you to jot down your own thoughts as you go through *LEAD NOW!*

The idea icon means "action plan." It appears in two places: (1) the action plan "prep" sections (places designed to help you explore concepts related to an action plan), and (2) the action plans themselves.

The change to this edition over the first edition is that now this book is a complete handbook for achieving the results you desire and that you are responsible for. Your challenge is to develop your capabilities, talents, and skills so that you move to the next level in any endeavor you attempt!

Section I

Included in this section is an introduction to our Leadership Development approach—focusing on one "fleck of gold" at a time. Also, it explains the background of the *LEAD NOW! Model* and guidance on how to build an effective Action Plan for improving your leadership capacity.

Chapter One
How to Use LEAD NOW!

The story is told of a Boston merchant in 1849 who was caught up in the California gold rush fever. He sold his Boston store and all his possessions and trekked across America to the gold fields of California to seek his fortune. He had dreams of the rivers in California being filled with gold nuggets so big that they could barely be carried. Day after endless day, the young man dipped his pan into the river and came up empty. His only reward was a growing pile of rocks. Discouraged and broke, he was ready to quit. However, one day an old, experienced prospector said to him, "That's quite a pile of rocks you got there, my boy."

The young man replied, "There's no gold here. I'm going back home. I'm finished."

Walking over to the pile of rocks, the old wise prospector said, "Oh, there's gold all right in these dirty rocks. You just have to know where to find it." The old timer then picked up two of the rocks from the pile and smashed them together. One of the rocks split open, revealing several flecks of gold sparkling in the sunlight.

Noticing a bulging leather pouch fastened to the prospector's waist, the young man said, "No, I'm not looking for flecks of gold. I'm looking for large chunks of gold like the ones you have in your pouch!"

The old prospector extended his pouch toward the

young man, who looked inside expecting several large shiny nuggets, but was stunned to see that the pouch was filled with thousands of small flecks of gold.

The old prospector said, "Son, it seems to me you are so busy looking for large nuggets that you're missing filling your pouch with these precious flecks of gold. The patient accumulation of these little flecks has brought me great wealth."[1]

It is our experience from coaching hundreds of leaders that too often leaders are looking for a single experience that will vault them to success; the unique moment that qualifies them as a complete leader. But like the Boston merchant, they misunderstand how true leadership is created. Real and lasting improvements in one's skill level and leadership talents are developed one small step at a time. From small and simple things, major gains occur.

The great hotel founder of Marriott Hotels, J. Willard Marriott, expressed his personal philosophy of management: "You can't improve 1000 percent in one thing, but you can improve 1 percent in a thousand things." Over the course of his successful career, Mr. Marriott learned the same lesson that the old prospector learned, that it takes many small "flecks" patiently yet persistently acquired over time to add up to the desired level of performance.

The same is true in one's desire to become a solid and trusted leader—whether in industry, teaching, business, community, parenting, church, school, coaching, medicine, law, science, art, music, military, athletics, or any endeavor. It is unrealistic to expect large, major leaps of progress over night. The truth is that it takes persistent, patient effort over time to see and experience gains in one's ability to lead—one fleck at a time.

Background

LEAD NOW! was created to help leaders develop the tools to identify and improve their ability to lead and coach others at a moment's notice. This book is filled with hundreds of small golden flecks—called *tips*—divided across twenty-one Leadership Dimensions that are designed to help any leader in any field grow in his or her ability to lead more effectively—one "fleck" at a time.

Becoming an agile, flexible leader requires easily-accessible leadership development tools. *LEAD NOW!* provides a user-friendly and complete action guide for leaders at every level of the organization.

LEAD NOW! consists of three parts:

1. The *LEAD NOW! Leadership Model* and leadership exercises

2. *Leadership Dimensions*, each with quotes, tips, resource references, self-assessment questions, and action planning notes for a busy leader

3. *Action Planning* reflection pages, exercises, and templates for leaders and their people

The content for *LEAD NOW!* comes primarily from two sources: 1) the authors' extensive organizational consulting and coaching experiences, and 2) proprietary 360-degree and team effectiveness assessments performed over the last three decades. Clients have included organizations and leaders from a host of government agencies, Fortune 500 companies, and government contractors in the aerospace, defense, technology, energy, electronics, software, and communications industries.

Several assumptions and beliefs form the foundation for *LEAD NOW!*:

- Leadership is critical to an organization's performance
- Leaders can and should be developed
- Organizations benefit by investing in developing and retaining good leaders
- Leadership development requires significant, specific, and focused effort
- Development without support and follow up produces little to no change

Leadership is a future-oriented ability to establish direction, align people, and help others to work together. We believe a leader is one who develops a vision of the future, prepares the strategies for achieving it, and supports the execution of that vision.

We also strongly believe that the ability to develop and execute the *what* and the *how* of vision resides in basic leadership behaviors. Identifying and improving these specific behaviors will increase the success of leading.

We are excited to share this leadership model with you. We are confident it will build your ability to lead others!

Successful Action Planning Tips

As you read through this handbook, think about your own development, and create your Action Plan with the following tips in mind:

1. Select something you have a desire to change or to develop.
   - *WHY*: Without a desire to change, you will likely not stick with it.

2. Only work on 2 or 3 areas at a time.
   - *WHY*: Having too many priorities often means no priorities.

3. Identify 1 to 3 measurable activities for each area.
   - *WHY*: Goals without performance measures rarely succeed.

4. Leverage your strengths and minimize the impact of your weaknesses.
   - *WHY*: Most professionals succeed by using their strengths. Excessive focus on weaknesses erodes and dilutes your powerful strengths.

5. Be very specific and concrete about areas you wish to improve or focus on.
   - *WHY*: Specific, concrete details will keep you focused on your goals.

6. Start with small changes and then progress to larger changes.
   - *WHY*: The only way to eat an elephant is by taking many small bites.

7. Identify roadblocks that may prevent the development plan from happening.
   - *WHY*: Every path to success has potholes, speed bumps, and road blocks; anticipate and prepare for them if you want to reach your goal.

8. Consider creating ways to work around your weaknesses by utilizing others' strengths—building your team to offset your shortcomings or delegating tasks to others with strengths that you don't have.
   - *WHY*: A key function of a team is to mold strengths and weaknesses of all members so that collectively the team achieves true synergy.

9. Select people to follow up with you—a mentor, boss, consultant, coach, peer, or friend.
   - *WHY*: Your motivation and willpower will fluctuate; working with a partner will strengthen both.
10. Tell others what your development plan is—the more you share your plan, the greater the chance it will happen.
    - *WHY*: Establishing external expectations and accountability will help you stay committed in moments of vacillation.
11. Learn from watching or reading about others who excel in the areas you wish to develop.
    - *WHY*: You can avoid pitfalls and gain valuable insights by learning from others who have mastered the areas you are working on.
12. Remember you can't be amazing at everything.
    - *WHY*: You are human; give yourself a break.
13. Celebrate successes along the way.
    - *WHY*: Small celebrations recharge your commitment.

Endnote
1. M. Russell Ballard, *Ensign*, May 2011

Notes

Section II

Included in this Section is the *LEAD NOW! Model* along with the *Leadership Dimensions* associated within each Quadrant. Each *Leadership Dimension* is also defined with extensive Tips, References, Self-assessment Questions, and Action Planning Notes for immediate application.

Chapter Two
LEAD NOW! Model

The first step in developing your leadership ability is to identify your leadership focus areas. This involves a process of defining the gaps between your capabilities today and what you are interested in doing differently in the future. This will involve leveraging a strength or overcoming a skill- or attitude-based challenge.

To help you identify your leadership focus areas, we have developed the *LEAD NOW! Leadership Development Model*. It is a practical and results-based approach for developing leaders. The most effective leaders build their leadership capability in each of the model's four quadrants.

LEAD NOW! MODEL

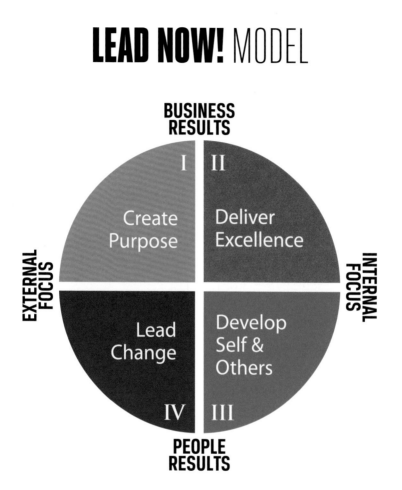

Quadrant I: Create Purpose

(Externally Focused Business Results)

A leader is responsible for defining the group's vision and strategy. Creating Purpose identifies what the organization stands for, what it is going to do, and how it is positioned in the marketplace. This involves studying the competition, thoroughly knowing the customer, analyzing industry trends, setting strategy, and communicating effectively to others.

Quadrant II: Deliver Excellence

(Internally Focused Business Results)

A leader is responsible for delivering operational excellence—translating the strategy into day-to-day execution for the organization. This involves clear decision making, the ability to build consistent and measurable processes, continuous improvement, and behaving with integrity.

Quadrant III: Develop Self & Others

(Internally Focused People Results)

A leader must value learning for him/herself and for others. This involves seeking personal improvement opportunities, building and managing team dynamics, honing technical expertise, managing one's time, coaching and developing others, and managing one's ego.

Quadrant IV: Lead Change

(Externally Focused People Results)

A leader is responsible for creating and championing change efforts that will benefit the organization. This involves influencing key decision makers, sponsoring change projects, empowering stakeholders, encouraging innovation, managing resistance, and making change stick.

Self-assessment

Consider your personal leadership development in each of the four quadrants of the *LEAD NOW! Model*. Refer back to the model and rate your understanding and skill in each quadrant using the following scale:

Poor   Excellent

1   2   3   4   5   6   7

	Score		Score
Quad I		**Quad III**	
Quad II		**Quad IV**	

What trends do you see? Which section(s) of the model stands out?

Comments:

Leadership Dimensions Overview

To help you in your leadership development, we break down the model into smaller parts. Each area of the model has several Leadership Dimensions. These Leadership Dimensions are listed below and are discussed in the next chapter.

LEAD NOW! MODEL
21 Leadership Dimensions

BUSINESS RESULTS

CREATE PURPOSE
DELIVER EXCELLENCE

EXTERNAL FOCUS
INTERNAL FOCUS

I
1. Customer Focus
2. Effective Communication
3. Presentation Skills
4. Strategic Thinking

II
5. Decision Making
6. Delegating
7. Dependability
8. Focusing on Results
9. Personal Integrity
10. Problem Solving

IV
18. Change Management
19. Innovation
20. Inspiring Commitment
21. Organizational Savvy

III
11. Coaching
12. Ego Management
13. Listening
14. Personal Development
15. Team Building
16. Time Management
17. Valuing Others

LEAD CHANGE
DEVELOP SELF & OTHERS

PEOPLE RESULTS

Quadrant I: Create Purpose
1. Customer Focus
2. Effective Communication
3. Presentation Skills
4. Strategic Thinking

Quadrant II: Deliver Excellence
5. Decision Making
6. Delegating
7. Dependability
8. Focusing on Results
9. Personal Integrity
10. Problem Solving

Quadrant III: Develop Self & Others
11. Coaching
12. Ego Management
13. Listening
14. Personal Development
15. Team Building
16. Time Management
17. Valuing Others

Quadrant IV: Lead Change
18. Change Management
19. Innovation
20. Inspiring Commitment
21. Organizational Savvy

Self-assessment

As you briefly review the Leadership Dimensions, compete an initial, quick self-assessment. Use the following scale to "evaluate" your mastery of each dimension.

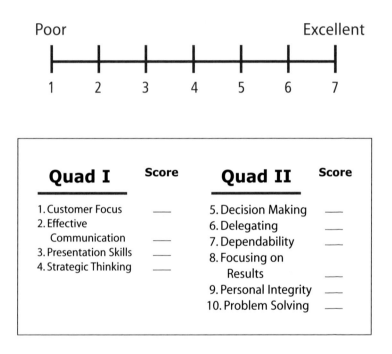

Poor   Excellent

1   2   3   4   5   6   7

Quad I	Score	**Quad II**	Score
1. Customer Focus	—	5. Decision Making	—
2. Effective Communication	—	6. Delegating	—
3. Presentation Skills	—	7. Dependability	—
4. Strategic Thinking	—	8. Focusing on Results	—
		9. Personal Integrity	—
		10. Problem Solving	—

Comments:

Quad III	Score	Quad IV	Score
11. Coaching	___	18. Change Management	___
12. Ego Management	___		
13. Listening	___	19. Innovation	___
14. Personal Development	___	20. Inspiring Commitment	___
15. Team Building	___		
16. Time Management	___	21. Organizational Savvy	___
17. Valuing Others	___		

Comments:

What trends do you see? Which dimensions in the model stand out? Your highest-rated dimensions represent strengths you should leverage, while your lowest-rated could be improved.

Reflection

It is common for leaders to feel comfortable in one area and not in another. For example, some may excel in developing business strategy and yet struggle in adjusting their leadership style in developing others. Other leaders may feel more comfortable championing a change effort, but have difficulty defining a process.

This assessment will become your "baseline"—the starting point for measurable growth and sustainable change in your leadership behaviors.

Leadership Goal Worksheet

At the end of this book, we have included Action Plan templates to help you make a plan for improved leadership. As a preparation for formalizing those action plans, we have included the following questions to help you identify why you need to improve, your desire to change, and your initial thoughts regarding how and/or what to change.

1. From your initial self-assessments (refer to pages 13, 16, and 17), write down the *LEAD NOW!* quadrants and the leadership dimensions that you would like to focus on (select 3-5 items initially).

2. What do I need to develop, improve, or change?

3. Why do I feel the need to change this? What could be the cause of this need?

4. How will I make this a priority?

Chapter Three
21 Leadership Dimensions

Use these Leadership Dimensions to build and implement your action plan.

Each Leadership Dimension includes:
- A Thought-provoking Quote
- Ready-to-Use Tips
- Resource References
- Self-assessment Questions
- Action Planning Notes

The Leadership Dimensions are organized by *LEAD NOW!* quadrant. We chose this approach to emphasize the relationship between dimensions and results and to help you quickly identify which dimensions you should focus on for the results you want. Page numbers are included for easy reference.

Dimension 1: Customer Focus

"Take care of your customer or somebody else will."

— Anonymous

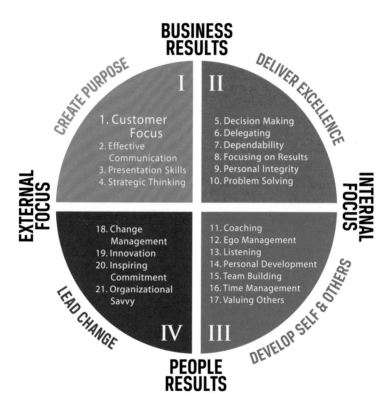

Overview

Peter Drucker taught us that a customer is anyone who can tell you no. We have been taught for years how the customer is king. Combine these two thoughts and it becomes apparent that no business can succeed without a constant awareness and courting of the customer. You and your team must be in touch with both your internal *and* external customers. They are the lifeblood of your business. Nurture them. Study them. Learn from them. Stay close to them. Never take them for granted. Act with the customer in mind. Train your team to get first hand information and use it for improvements in your organization. Balancing their demands is a difficult dance.

To help you be more effective in your customer focus, consider the following tips:

Tips

1. You have both internal and external customers.

   - Internal customers are the people or departments within your organization who rely on your service or product.
   - External customers are people outside your organization who purchase your services or products.

2. Both external and internal customers are vital to your success. They both have needs that deserve to be heard, acknowledged, and met. You take care of them and they are yours. Treat them poorly or take them for granted and they will go elsewhere.

3. Former customers can provide valuable insights into their previous experience with your firm. They can give you feedback on your strengths, weaknesses, and why they left you.

4. Increased customer satisfaction is the result of relating to your customers. Get into their shoes and learn their perspective of what it is like to work with you from every aspect.

5. Frequently solicit both formal and informal feedback from your customers on how you are doing.

6. Identify your customers' expectations. Learn what they truly want and how they want it.

7. Never take your customers for granted. They can change tastes on a whim. You must keep up.

8. It is good to be aware of previous experience, but do not rely on it too much—it cannot accurately predict the future. Too many new variables come into play.

9. Study your competition. Examine what they are doing well and where they are slipping. Learn from their experiences—past and present. What is their standing in the marketplace? Analyze where they are and why.

10. Establish key points of contact among your customers. You will be able to rely on them for information, opinions, perceptions, suggestions, and general feedback. Use them as sounding boards to try out new ideas. Ask their opinion on challenges you face.

11. The single most effective way to build a strong relationship with a customer is through honest, effective, ongoing communication.

12. When a mistake happens, level with your customers. Don't hide it. Be forthright. They will likely work with you. But, if you are not honest and straight with them, their level of trust in you can be severely damaged. It all comes down to trust!

13. Good listening skills are critical in establishing a relationship with your customers. They want and need to be heard. The amount of listening you provide is far more important than the amount of talking you give.

14. Your customers will judge you on your attitude toward them, toward yourself, and toward your team and organization. You cannot hide your attitude from them.

15. When there is a problem, involve them in fixing it. If you do this, they are likely to ask you for help in solving future problems they will have. You can turn a problem into a classic "win-win" situation.

16. The most important rule to remember in effectively dealing with a customer is: *listen*!

17. Create a partnership with your customer interface/ representative.

18. Meet frequently to clarify, assess and improve your performance and deliverables.

19. Beware of relying on distant/remote sources for information. Deal directly with the customer.

20. Be honest. Be specific. Be proactive.

21. It is always better that the customer learns of job difficulties from you than from others.

22. Inform the customer of problems or setbacks in a timely manner. Not keeping a customer up-to-date can promote distrust and suspicion.

23. Use customer feedback religiously and fully.

24. Regard any complaint as a customer gift.

25. Remember you can't be all things to all people.

26. Aftermarketing is the key to keeping customers for life.

27. Though it might be trite, it's still true: "Go the extra mile." This is especially true for tough customers.

28. Meet the schedule you committed to. If you can't, don't surprise your customer.

29. "Use your good judgment in all situations." (Nordstrom philosophy in dealing with customers.)

30. Know your customers *and* let your customers know you.

31. Do not try to impress your customers with a dazzling array of complexity. Sell them on the simple ideas they want to buy.

32. When you've made the sale, stop talking.

33. Identify and prioritize future customer needs.

34. Be comfortable and responsive to customer complaints.

35. Think of yourself as a dissatisfied customer. What would you do to fix things?

36. Remember: customers complain—it's their job.

References

Total Customer Service; William H. Davidow and Bro Uttal, Harper Perennial, 1990.

Achieving Excellence Through Customer Service; John Tschohl, Prentice-Hall, 1991.

Building A Chain of Customers; Richard J. Schonberger, Free Press, 1990.

The Spirit to Serve: Marriott's Way; J.W. Marriott Jr., Kathi Ann Brown, Harper Perennial, 1997.

Raving Fans: A Revolutionary Approach to Customer Service; Ken Blanchard and Sheldon Bowles, Morrow, 1993.

Customers for Life : How to Turn That One-Time Buyer into a Lifetime Customer; Carl Sewell, Paul B. Brown, Bantam Books, 2002.

Creating Competitive Advantage: Give Customers a Reason to Choose You Over Your Competitors; Jaynie L. Smith, William Flanagan, Doubleday Publishing, 2006.

Moments of Truth; Jan Carlzon, Collins Business, 1989.

Self-assessment

 Using the scale provided, rate yourself on the following leadership behaviors.

Poor   Excellent

1   2   3   4   5   6   7

_____ I am focused on the needs of the customer.

_____ I know the needs of each of my customer groups.

_____ I plan my business based on my customers' needs.

_____ I review my business based on my customers' needs.

_____ I analyze information about my customers.

_____ I gather feedback from my customers.

Action Planning Notes

 What three things in this section will help you be a better leader?

1.

2.

3.

What would change if you started or continued doing these three things?

How can you implement these changes?

Dimension 2: Effective Communication

"The biggest hurdle to effective communication is the assumption that it has taken place."

— Anonymous

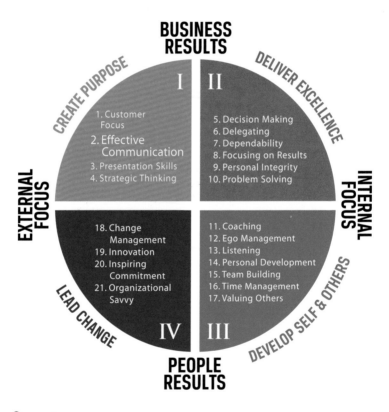

BUSINESS RESULTS

CREATE PURPOSE

DELIVER EXCELLENCE

I
1. Customer Focus
2. Effective Communication
3. Presentation Skills
4. Strategic Thinking

II
5. Decision Making
6. Delegating
7. Dependability
8. Focusing on Results
9. Personal Integrity
10. Problem Solving

EXTERNAL FOCUS

INTERNAL FOCUS

IV
18. Change Management
19. Innovation
20. Inspiring Commitment
21. Organizational Savvy

III
11. Coaching
12. Ego Management
13. Listening
14. Personal Development
15. Team Building
16. Time Management
17. Valuing Others

LEAD CHANGE

DEVELOP SELF & OTHERS

PEOPLE RESULTS

Overview

Communication is the lifeblood of an organization. Every aspect of the business relies on the effective exchange of information. Your role as an effective communicator cannot be adequately emphasized. The only way you can lead others is to communicate with them. This same skill applies directly to the relationships you develop with your supervisors, peers, customers, vendors, and all stakeholders. The degree to which you develop your communication skills will directly determine your overall success as a leader and as a professional.

To help you be more effective in your communication, consider the following tips:

Tips

1. Be seen as a person who eagerly shares information with your associates in a timely and honest manner.

2. Discover specifically what your teammates and associates *need* to know. Also learn what they *want* to know. That will help prioritize information flow.

3. Never shoot the messenger. Reinforce them for their honesty and forthrightness. This will ensure that you are not kept out of the loop in the future.

4. An effective team works in a climate of open information exchange with each other, across departments, and across the organization.

5. Ask your boss how he or she wants to be kept informed (how often, how much detail, by what method, and by whom). Have a frank discussion to learn his or her definition of "urgent." This needs to be clarified to help you respond. Further clarify your boss' priorities and how these affect your responses.

6. Interact willingly, directly, and openly. This builds trust and dependability. Both are essential for productive performance.

7. Identify key people in the organization that you should keep fully or partially informed, and follow through.

8. Analyze communication breakdowns. Why have they occurred? How can they be prevented in the future? Involve others in your analysis. They are part of the solution.

9. Remember that no one likes surprises.

10. Identify potential communication breakdowns and plan methods to prevent them.

11. Make sure your meetings are not one-way data dumping sessions. Encourage open exchanges to increase communication and hear all sides of each agenda item. When one individual dominates a discussion it may be that others fear to disagree, are confused, or there was no need for discussion in the first place.

12. Appoint a "recorder" in your meetings. Keep track of "action items."

13. Email and texting are tremendous tools. However, they should not replace necessary face-to-face or phone interactions. For significant interactions, consciously determine the best method to employ. Suggest to your team that they use the same analysis.

14. Briefly review each day who should be informed of special or unusual items.

15. It is generally obvious that we should inform people of new developments. But people also appreciate knowing that there are no new developments.

16. Plan "Managing By Walking Around" (MBWA) times into your schedule to stay informed. These informal chats are very worthwhile opportunities to exchange

information. They also allow you to feel the pulse of the organization, listen to opinions, and learn of concerns.

17. Seek the opinion of others to determine the best methods to keep your people informed. Frequently ask for feedback on the effectiveness of the techniques.

18. Involve your people in establishing an electronic or physical bulletin board for work and personal items of interest.

19. Be timely in giving people information that affects them. Your team also needs to know the information that indirectly affects them (i.e., information regarding departments your team interacts with).

20. Explain WHY a request is urgent. Your people will respond far better when they understand the "why."

21. Be careful of messages that you send nonverbally. Ask for feedback and clarification.

22. Try to understand before you worry about being understood.

23. Communicate your feelings without putting the other person down. When you disagree with a person, be sure you express your view without demeaning or attacking the other person.

24. Use both verbal and written directions and instructions.

25. Coach your employees to communicate information they need to complete tasks and assignments they have. Be open and responsive to their inputs and questions. Never let them feel it is a bother to you or they will stop communicating with you.

26. When communicating to others—especially one-on-one—give them 100 percent of your attention. They are watching, far more than you will ever realize, to see if you do or do not listen to them.

27. As a leader, everything you say is "on the record." Others pay attention to *everything you* say whether you are at a restaurant, a bar, in the office, on a business trip, or at a social gathering. Be on your guard. Whatever you say to your people or to others is usually interpreted as an official statement.

28. After giving directions, ask for a restatement of the directions to ensure correct understanding.

29. Healthy organizations require a great deal of free-flowing information, up, down, and across the organization.

30. Attack the problem, not the person.

31. If the "how" is important to you, then the effort to clarify the "how" must be equally important.

32. Remember, when you think you've communicated enough, double it.

33. Watch for conflicted messages. When they occur, deal with them immediately.

34. Suspend judgment as you listen to others.

35. Put down your mobile device when listening.

36. Employees always want their boss to follow-up and follow through; just like bosses want the same from their employees.

37. Nonverbal messages speak loudly. In fact, nonverbal cues are a more accurate representation of the message than the verbal content. People will believe the

messages your non-verbal gestures are sending above the messages your words are sending.

38. Remember to tune into the nonverbal messages others send while you are talking with them.

39. Keys to communication with your people:

- Honest
- Ongoing
- Appropriate
- Clear and concise
- Timely

References

Messages: The Communication Skills Book; Matthew McKay, Patrick Fanning, Martha Davis, New Harbinger, 1995.

People Skills; Robert Bolton, Touchstone, 1986.

Crucial Conversations: Tools for Talking When Stakes are High; Kerry Patterson, Joseph Grenny, Ron McMillan, Al Switzler, McGraw-Hill, 2002.

The Art and Science of Communication: Tools for Effective Communication in the Workplace; P. S. Perkins, Wiley, 2008.

101 Ways to Improve Your Communication Skills Instantly; Bennie Bough, GoalMinds, Inc., 2005.

The Art of Talking So That People Will Listen: Getting Through to Family, Friends and Business Associates; Paul W. Swets, Fireside, 1986.

Self-assessment

 Using the scale provided, rate yourself on the following leadership behaviors.

Poor   Excellent

1   2   3   4   5   6   7

_____ I listen for understanding before I respond.

_____ I keep stakeholders up-to-date.

_____ I balance my use of email, texting, instant messaging, face-to-face, and phone communications.

_____ I ask open-ended questions and allow space for others to respond.

_____ I am concise and clear in my communication.

_____ I stay on message when addressing a group.

Comments:

Action Planning Notes

 What three things in this section will help you be a better leader?

1.

2.

3.

What would change if you started or continued doing these three things?

How can you implement these changes?

Dimension 3: Presentation Skills

"Regardless of the changes in technology, the market for
well-crafted messages will always have an audience"

— Steve Burnett

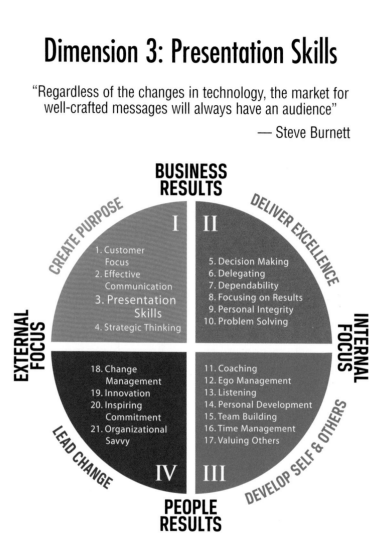

Overview

Presenting in front of an audience of your peers and associates is, for most individuals, an unusual opportunity to let others know of your talents, thinking, and potential. You will have the chance to let others know you, your ideas, and the force of your personality, as well as your potential for bigger responsibility. For some, weekly presentations become a standard part of their job. For the prepared, giving a presentation can be a huge career enhancer by establishing yourself as a solid professional and leader. To help you be more effective in your presentation skills, consider the following tips:

Tips

1. Identify what you want your audience to take away from your presentation.

2. Identify biases and specific attitudes of those in your audience. Anticipate their concerns, hot buttons, and questions.

3. Have a grabber to open your presentation. Grabbers can include photos, stories, dramatic examples, comparisons, statistics, or personal experiences. Consider your audience as you choose what you will use.

4. Use a strong closing sentence to create a lasting impression.

5. Make sure the audience can answer:
   - "Why do I care?"
   - "Why would I want that?"
   - "How will it help me, my team, and the company?"
   - "Is there anything new here?"
   - "What's in it for me?"

6. Show how each thought, idea or action will be beneficial.

7. Summarize your real purpose in one sentence and repeat it at the beginning and at the conclusion.

8. Does your presentation include a "call to action"? If so, make it clear, especially at the end.

9. Tell them what you are going to say, say it, and tell them what you have said.

10. Speak on subjects you know. Otherwise it will be apparent and will damage your credibility and reputation.

11. Remember, the audience will be asking "*so what?*"

12. Your audience needs to feel your energy and enthusiasm. They will usually remember that long after your words are forgotten.

13. Anticipate questions. Build the answers into the content of your presentation.

14. As you prepare your content, group your ideas under natural headings. Each heading should support your over-arching purpose.

15. Communicate using the language of the people you are addressing.

16. Your presentation should be relevant, purposeful, and direct.

17. Jokes and humor can be risky. Humor often backfires and is misunderstood—making you look foolish. Use it carefully.

18. Know if your audience prefers numbers or words.

19. Keep it brief.

20. Powerpoint presentations can be effective, but only if they are used properly. Poorly designed Powerpoint presentations can lock you in and prevent you from responding to audience reactions. If you use Power-

point, learn the best ways to use it to augment your presentation and allow yourself the flexibility to delve deeper when needed in response to your audience.

21. Know the room you will be in. Become familiar with the layout: size, shape, external noise, windows, sunlight, podium, tables, lighting, riser to stand on, AV and other equipment, furniture arrangement, and microphone.

22. Practice! Privately rehearse your delivery *out loud*. Just reading it to yourself does not allow your mouth and tongue to become familiar with the phrases you need to emphasize.

23. Nervousness is natural and expected. It is also essential. Nervousness brings energy, conviction, and animation. It just needs to be channeled and managed. The audience responds to energy, and they go to sleep without it.

24. A reliable test for your preparation is to ask yourself what the average audience member will remember 30 minutes after hearing your presentation.

25. If possible, record your rehearsals so you can see what you really look like while giving the presentation. Video feedback never lies.

26. Never give the same speech to different audiences. Audiences differ. Study each audience's makeup, background, level of sophistication, education, concerns, friendliness, and emotions.

27. What techniques will you use to hold your audience's attention?

28. Remain cool when challenged and when controversial topics arise. Never be defensive.

29. Later, ask others for feedback about your presentation.

30. Adjust your tone, pace, and style to the audience.

31. Be sensitive to people's time and do not go over. Use a few minutes less than the allotted time.

32. Avoid distracting non-verbal gestures or questionable electronic malfunction issues. Other distractions include pocket change and keys.

33. Do not do anything to distract your audience from the main message.

34. Manage your nerves (breathe deeply, drink water, finger and hand isometrics, etc.)

35. Ensure that the room is prepared.

36. Be likable—that is the #1 element that people look for.

37. Establish credibility.

38. Your final impression is a lasting one. You are the one "on stage." How you look, how you carry yourself, how you speak—all make up that final impression.

References

Leading Out Loud: Inspiring Change Through Authentic Communications; Terry Pearce, Jossey-Bass, 2003.

The Elements of Great Public Speaking; J. Lyman MacInnis, Ten Speed Press, 2006.

Crucial Conversations: Tools for Talking when Stakes are High; Kerry Patterson, Joseph Grenny, Ron McMillan, Al Switzler McGraw-Hill, 2002.

How to Prepare, Stage, and Deliver Winning Presentations; Thomas Leech, AMACOM, 2004.

———◆———

Presentation Zen: Simple Ideas on Presentation Design and Delivery; Garr Reynolds, New Riders Press, 2008.

The Exceptional Presenter: A Proven Formula to Open Up and Own the Room; Timothy J. Koegel, Greenleaf Book Group Press, 2007.

Presenting to Win: The Art of Telling Your Story; Jerry Weissman, Prentice Hall, 2006.

Beyond Bullet Points: Using Microsoft® Office PowerPoint® 2007 to Create Presentations That Inform, Motivate, and Inspire; Cliff Atkinson, Microsoft Press, 2007.

Self-assessment

 Using the scale provided, rate yourself on the following leadership behaviors.

Poor   Excellent

1   2   3   4   5   6   7

_____ I adjust my presentation based on the audience.

_____ I am clear about my main message.

_____ I am clear about my desired outcomes.

_____ I use metaphors or stories to illustrate major points.

_____ I practice, practice, practice.

_____ I avoid reading the material.

_____ I am prepared and confident responding to questions.

Action Planning Notes

 What three things in this section will help you be a better leader?

1.

2.

3.

What would change if you started or continued doing these three things?

How can you implement these changes?

Dimension 4: Strategic Thinking

"The best way to predict the future is to create it."

— Peter Drucker

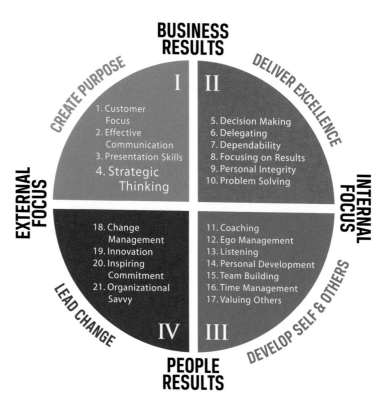

Overview

You, as a leader, need to think strategically. You must analyze problems, challenges, and opportunities from a broad—*big picture*—perspective. Then you anticipate and plan for the reactions of any and all variables that may have an affect on your vision. You can then focus team energies and capabilities on *key* actions that will maximize your advantage to the organization. Successful strategic capabilities are characterized by your being able to visualize daily tactical approaches and responses to both anticipated and unexpected issues that surface along the way. This is the essence of sound and admired leadership in meeting goals and targets. Effective strategic practitioners are in a class by themselves.

To help you be more effective as a strategic thinker, consider the following tips:

Tips

1. Thinking strategically means shifting away from day-to-day firefighting.

2. Strong leaders think strategically by looking at opportunities and issues from a broader perspective. Then they anticipate and plan for possible reactions to them. These reactions may come from the marketplace, analysts, industry observers, outsiders, insiders, associates, and stakeholders.

3. When making a decision that affects your organization, consider both short-term effects and long-term ramifications.

4. Strategic thinking is relative to your sphere of influence. Tailor it to your needs and scope.

5. Regularly read business journals, newspapers, and electronic reports; listen to interviews and media reports; stay current, follow futurists, and pay attention to market trends. Ask yourself how all this information influences the decisions you make.

6. Assess your personal risk tendencies on a risk spectrum ranging from "risk avoidance" to "risk seeking."

7. Don't look for a quick fix to address problems. Instead, take advantage of this window of opportunity by looking at the broader context in considering possible options and new directions. Be open to non-traditional solutions.

8. Discuss some of your challenges with those who are formally working in strategic endeavors or initiatives in your organization. Solicit their ideas. Have them teach you their views and methods.

9. Periodically discuss business strategies with your boss or other senior managers to develop a feel for the organization's status and future (near and long term).

10. Identify the paradigms and attitudes that your team is currently operating under. Then decide if any of them are antiquated or obsolete. Should any be replaced, redefined, or reinforced?

11. Identify what critical success factors you need for your group to be effective.

12. Look at your organization from the perspective of your regular customers. The customer is the center point of the business. What do you see? What understanding does this new vantage point give you?

13. Get a greater sense of your organization by looking at it from a 500-foot perspective, and then a 50,000-foot perspective. Notice how the higher you go, the broader your view becomes—allowing you to remove yourself from the basic functions and appreciate the entire operation. With this view, you are moving from "tactical" to "strategic" in your thinking.

14. Be aware of the financial condition (overview) and general budget issues of the company. Have a greater awareness of your own department's financial situation and its impact on the entire organization.

15. Design a detailed analysis of each of your organization's major competitors. Examine comparative metrics. How does your company fit in? Where does it excel? Where does it need strengthening?

16. Involve your own group. Solicit ideas and views from them in developing strategies for:
    - Customer Focus
    - Risk
    - Group Direction
    - Change
    - Group Support

17. When reviewing the health or direction of a project or program, consider the schedule and its impact on the budget, on customer relations, and on your people's performance and support.

18. Pay attention to how all the functional groups in your organization affect each other. What purposes and coordinated efforts do they have beyond the obvious? Think about those relationships. Where are the hand-off points? What are the most essential linkages?

19. Think like a CEO.

20. Develop a team of the willing and able.

21. Consider how the stakeholder views it.

22. Always seek for global "best practices."

23. Stay current on new developments, improvements, and alterations to processes, systems, and methods.

Analyze the reasons for the changes and how you can take advantage of them.

24. Have market sense of how to grow the business.

25. Remember that nothing is sacred:

- Question the ways your team deals with challenges, issues, problems, and decisions.
- Challenge old assumptions and belief systems that your organization operates within.
- Review all elements and factors that stifle greater performance. Are they necessary? Why are they there?
- Look at all relationships you and your team have. Are they relevant? What value do they bring?
- How do you run the business? How do you manage transactions? Are your methods relevant today? Should they be improved? Do you take full advantage of new technologies?

26. Seek to create a world-class organization.

27. Break problems apart into smaller pieces.

28. Pay attention to details; they support the over-arching purpose of your organization.

29. Question the status quo.

30. Identify measures and targets for each initiative and program.

31. Debate, process, and discuss issues.

32. Consider the difference between:

- intuitive thinking
- conceptual thinking
- critical thinking
- creative thinking

Each of these four thinking skills is essential to being an effective strategist.

33. Be willing to make trade-offs and take risks.

34. Make the tough calls and choices.

35. Display an attitude that we can implement new ways of doing business.

36. Question traditional methods and look for new opportunities.

37. Effective strategic thinking requires that you consider each of the following:
    - demographics
    - logistics
    - vendors and suppliers
    - customer needs and demands
    - technology (current and future)
    - competitors
    - resources (available and unavailable)
    - regulations
    - workforce

References

Competitive Strategy: Techniques for Analyzing Industries and Competitors; Michael E. Porter, Free Press, 1998.

Corporate Life Cycles: How and Why Corporations Grow and Die and What to Do About It; Ichak Adizes, Prentice-Hall, 1990.

Management Challenges for the 21st Century; Peter F. Drucker, Harper Business, 1999.

Finance and Accounting for Nonfinancial Managers; William G. Droms, Addison-Wesley, 1990.

Organizational Capability: Competing From the Inside Out; Dave Ulrich, Dale Lake, Wiley & Sons, 1990.

Only the Paranoid Survive; Andrew S. Grove, Doubleday Business, 1999.

Good to Great: Why Some Companies Make the Leap . . . and Others Don't; Jim Collins, Collins Business, 2001.

Blue Ocean Strategy: How to Create Uncontested Market Space and Make Competition Irrelevant; W. Chan Kim, Renée Mauborgne, Harvard Business School Press, 2005.

Strategic Thinking: A Four Piece Puzzle; Bill Birnbaum, Douglas Mountain Publishing, 2004.

The Art and Practice of Leadership Coaching; Howard Morgan, Phil Hawkins, Marshall Goldsmith, John Wiley & Sons, 2005.

Champions of Change: How CEOs and their Companies are Mastering the Skills of Radical Change; David Nadler, Jossey-Boss, 1998.

What the CEO Wants You to Know; Ram Charan, Crown Business Books, 2001.

The First 90 Days: Critical Success Strategies for New Leaders at All Levels; Michael Watkins, Harvard Business School Press, 2003.

Self-assessment

 Using the scale provided, rate yourself on the following leadership behaviors.

Poor   Excellent

1   2   3   4   5   6   7

_____ I regularly scan outside market forces and competitive landscape.

_____ I regularly assess the current and future needs of our customers/stakeholders.

_____ I align initiatives to the needs of our customers/stakeholders.

_____ I regularly review and update our strategic direction and objectives.

_____ I use a scorecard to measure the success of business and people performance.

Comments:

Action Planning Notes

 What three things in this section will help you be a better leader?

1.

2.

3.

What would change if you started or continued doing these three things?

How can you implement these changes?

Dimension 5: Decision Making

"People who are denied the opportunity of making decisions of importance begin to regard as important the decisions they are allowed to take. They become fussy about filing, keen on seeing pencils sharpened and eager to ensure that the windows are opened."

— Prof. C.N. Parkinson

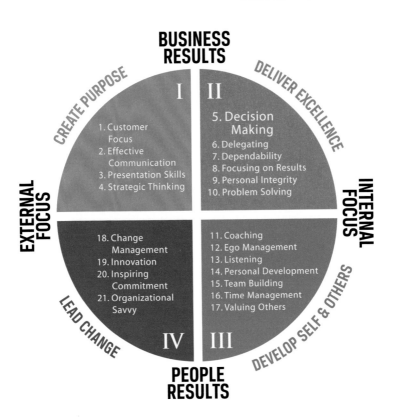

BUSINESS RESULTS

CREATE PURPOSE

DELIVER EXCELLENCE

I
1. Customer Focus
2. Effective Communication
3. Presentation Skills
4. Strategic Thinking

II
5. Decision Making
6. Delegating
7. Dependability
8. Focusing on Results
9. Personal Integrity
10. Problem Solving

EXTERNAL FOCUS

INTERNAL FOCUS

IV
18. Change Management
19. Innovation
20. Inspiring Commitment
21. Organizational Savvy

III
11. Coaching
12. Ego Management
13. Listening
14. Personal Development
15. Team Building
16. Time Management
17. Valuing Others

LEAD CHANGE

DEVELOP SELF & OTHERS

PEOPLE RESULTS

Overview

One of the toughest and yet most critical skills that a leader can possess is the ability to make wise decisions. Your goal is to make as many sound and solid decisions as possible. Your decisions will affect your career, the livelihood of your associates, the future of your organization, relationships with customers and vendors, and much, much more.

To help you be more effective in your decision making, consider the following tips (also see the tips in the "Problem Solving" section—many of them apply to decision making):

Tips

1. Time pressure and inadequate data are your two biggest hurdles in reaching a decision. They always will be, so you must be prepared to mitigate these factors.

2. Always consider asking trusted colleagues for opinions on the decision you are considering. They are more objective and will see it differently than you do. Never be so arrogant that you feel you do not need any help.

3. Be careful not to make your decision on assumptions that have not been tested. Unfortunately, many a faulty decision has been made when assumptions were foolishly considered to be facts.

4. When possible, consider sleeping on a decision to make sure it is your best choice. Let your brain work on it as you sleep.

5. At times, it is advantageous to delegate the decision to another. It may be a good developmental experi-

ence for your people. Have them report their thoughts and findings to see what they came up with and why.

6. Many tend to be forgetful. Identify a method of keeping track of your decisions.

7. Consult an associate who has faced a similar decision at some point. Find out what they did, how they made that decision, and what happened as a result.

8. Be cautious of excessive emotion as the decision is being made. Emotions can cloud the process, hinder the analysis, dilute the data, and distort the final outcome.

9. Some of the factors that contribute to poor decisions include: impatience, arrogance, limited perspective, faulty data, poor analysis, fear of risk, and not asking for help.

10. Beware of hasty decisions. Don't analyze or agonize excessively. You may end up waiting too long to decide. Find a healthy balance between haste and too much analysis.

11. Consider combining the most desirable aspects of two or more alternatives in making your decision.

12. Striving for consensus in a team is the ideal, but it is not mandatory and often is not realistic. Do not make the schedule suffer by indecisiveness because meeting after meeting still does not produce consensus. You, as the leader, must consequently make the call. Your team must then support the decision.

13. Mentally rehearse how the decision you are considering will actually play out if it is enacted. Visualize all aspects and possible consequences. Consider this step a dress rehearsal and a test of the final implementation.

14. The best decision is not always the first or second option. Don't stop there. Keep testing it until you finally get the highest quality decision possible.

15. Pay attention to your gut hunch as you consider the options available to you.

16. A vital and often overlooked aspect of decision making is implementation. This involves careful coordination of:
    - Announcement to those affected
    - Commitment of those involved
    - Resources needed
    - Schedule and timing
    - Responsibility

17. "No decision" should be viewed as a decision. It is an option and carries with it a message.

18. Recognize your track record in decision making. There are bound to be areas or subjects for which you make better decisions than others. Learn from your tendencies and act accordingly.

19. Gather as much data as your time allows when making a decision. Some tend to make decisions too quickly, without gathering enough data. Some tend to wait until all relevant data is gathered. Avoid both traps. Gather data, but recognize that when time runs out, you must make the call.

20. In a team decision making setting, dissent is imperative before the decision is made. However, once the debate ends, everyone must walk out of the room having whole-heartedly committed to support the decision.

21. Beware of perfectionist tendencies—no one can be right all the time. Don't wait for "perfect" decisions— they may never come.

22. People often make poor decisions when they are scared, anxious, or nervous. When making a decision, write down your fears and worries and categorize them. How legitimate are they?

23. Ask yourself how often you backpedal on decisions. Is there a trend?

24. Leaders must own the decision they are involved with even if they do not agree with the final decision.

25. Beware of decision *procrastination*—set up checkpoints along the way to keep you on track.

26. A team approach to decision making is best when:
    - You lack adequate information
    - The decision will directly affect the whole team
    - You need creative inputs
    - Time allows the team to confer
    - You will need the full team's support in the final decision and its implementation

27. A team decision is not needed when:
    - The decision is routine
    - Time does not allow for it
    - You honestly believe the majority will agree with you (use caution)
    - Buy-in is not necessary (use caution)
    - The team will support the outcome (use caution)

References

Heads You Win: How the Best Companies Think; Quinn Spitzer, Ron Evans, Simon & Schuster, 1997.

Making Judgments, Choices and Decisions In Business: Effective Management Through Self- Knowledge; Warren J. Keegan, John Wiley & Sons, 1984.

Whatever It Takes: Decision Makers at Work; Morgan W. McCall, Robert E. Kaplan, Prentice-Hall, 1985.

Getting Things Done: The Art of Stress-Free Productivity; David Allen, Viking Penguin, 2001.

Smart Choices: A Practical Guide to Making Better Decisions; John S. Hammond, Ralph L. Keeney, Howard Raiffa, Bantam Books, 2002.

Getting to Yes: Negotiating Agreement Without Giving In; Roger Fisher, Bruce M. Patton, William L. Ury, Houghton Mifflin, 1992.

Smart Choices: A Practical Guide to Making Better Decisions; John S. Hammond, Ralph L. Keeney, Howard Raiffa, Broadway, 2002.

How the Mighty Fall; Jim Collins, Random House, 2009.

Team of Rivals: The Political Genius of Abraham Lincoln; Doris Kearns Goodwin, Simon & Schuster, 2005.

Self-assessment

 Using the scale provided, rate yourself on the following leadership behaviors.

Poor   Excellent

1   2   3   4   5   6   7

_____ I use consensus to build buy-in and gather new ideas/perspectives.

_____ I manage my emotions during the decision making process.

_____ I am clear about when I should or should not make a decision.

_____ I avoid the tendency of ensuring perfection is reached before making a decision.

_____ I publicly own my decisions.

_____ I know when to stop analyzing a problem and make a decision.

Comments:

Action Planning Notes

 What three things in this section will help you be
a better leader?

1.

2.

3.

What would change if you started or continued doing these three things?

How can you implement these changes?

Dimension 6: Delegating

"The best executive is the one who has sense enough to pick good people to do what he wants done, and self-restraint enough to keep from meddling with them while they do it."

— Theodore Roosevelt

BUSINESS RESULTS

CREATE PURPOSE

I
1. Customer Focus
2. Effective Communication
3. Presentation Skills
4. Strategic Thinking

DELIVER EXCELLENCE

II
5. Decision Making
6. Delegating
7. Dependability
8. Focusing on Results
9. Personal Integrity
10. Problem Solving

EXTERNAL FOCUS

INTERNAL FOCUS

IV
18. Change Management
19. Innovation
20. Inspiring Commitment
21. Organizational Savvy

III
11. Coaching
12. Ego Management
13. Listening
14. Personal Development
15. Team Building
16. Time Management
17. Valuing Others

LEAD CHANGE

DEVELOP SELF & OTHERS

PEOPLE RESULTS

Overview

Successful delegating requires you to make a conscious choice to give up some of your own workload. This allows you to develop your people. Done well, delegating will result in a win-win for you *and* each of your people. In the process, you will dramatically augment your ability to do much more than you ever thought possible.

To help you be more effective as a delegator, consider the following tips:

Tips

1. The more effective the delegation, the more time the delegator will have to focus on other areas—especially higher priority items that are on your supervisor's agenda. These are called "career enhancers".

2. Effective delegation of assignments and tasks brings countless benefits to you and your people. It improves your time management, develops your people, and increases efficiency.

3. Delegation, as a skill, can be taught, learned, and developed.

4. When you delegate, look at obstacles—in advance—that can be problematic for the employee who will receive your delegated task. This will help you determine the amount of guidance he or she may need.

5. Not every employee requires the same style of delegation. You, as the leader, must consider their overall experience and their specific capacities related to the task you will delegate to them. Determining this at the beginning will save you considerable time in the long run.

6. Have contingency plans in place for high-priority delegated tasks in case a problem develops.

7. Support and encourage your people to make decisions and solve problems that affect the delegated task on their own. Challenge them to only involve you if they have reached their limit. This will develop and stretch them and will let you work on your own tasks.

8. The more time you spend clarifying the task and answering questions in the beginning, the less you will usually have to be involved later on. Clarity in the early stages is critical.

9. Be available for questions later on. However, be careful not to get too involved as you answer the questions. You may send the message that you don't trust them, or that you will do the job for them.

10. Be aware of the strengths, weaknesses, and capabilities of each of your people. This is essential to knowing which tasks to delegate to whom.

11. Make sure your employees have the needed training and exposure to the tasks they will be given.

12. When delegating, explain the *what* in detail, give them the *why*, but leave the *how* up to them.

13. There will be times when mistakes will be made by your people in performing delegated projects. Handled properly, these mistakes can turn into valuable coaching moments.

14. Analyze projects in the beginning by breaking them down into their basic functions and steps to see what skills and resources are required. This will help you determine who to assign to the project and what resources to provide. Try to match capabilities, per-

sonality traits, and thinking styles to the assigned tasks. Relationship skills also need to be considered.

15. A major challenge for newly-promoted leaders is to not do the task that they used to do. Delegate and let others do it. Leave them alone unless they need help.

16. Never feel threatened by your people for doing a job better than you could. You should *not* be able to do their job. You should just lead them and help them succeed.

17. Your job is to be the conductor of the orchestra. Each of your people should play their own part well. You need to see the big picture and how the separate parts come together. Playing their instruments for them is not your job.

18. Be open to your people discovering new ways to do their job. Encourage and support innovation.

19. When you delegate, don't hold a tight leash on your people, but don't abandon them either.

20. Encourage your people to give you periodic feedback on delegated projects. You cannot afford to be surprised.

21. Let them participate in setting their performance goals and areas of delegation. Give them the full story in terms of budget, deadlines, resources, previous lessons learned, customer demands, and management's direction.

22. Test a person's willingness and ability when delegating.

23. Don't assume communication has occurred. Seek confirmation.

24. Determine whether you need to provide the delegated task in writing—based upon previous performance.

25. Delegate not only responsibility but also accountability.

26. Avoid harsh criticism. Discuss poor job performance from a learning perspective.

27. Challenge them. Stretch them—gradually.

28. Remember the ability to delegate is what separates a manager from an individual contributor. If you don't delegate, you are not an effective manager. If you can't or won't delegate, then you've already plateaued.

29. A day is never more than 24 hours—delegation is the key to your effectiveness.

30. Delegation does not alleviate ultimate responsibility— follow-up is crucial.

31. Remember the higher up you go, the more you need other people.

References

If You Want It Done Right, You Don't Have to Do It Yourself: The Power of Effective Delegation; Donna M. Genett, Quill Driver Books, 2003.

Effective Delegation Skills; Bruce B. Tepper, AMI How-To Series, American Media Publishing, 1995.

The One Minute Manager Meets the Monkey; Kenneth H. Blanchard, William Oncken, Hal Burrows, Morrow & Company, 1991.

High Involvement Management; Edward Lawler, Jossey-Bass, 1987.

The Leadership Challenge: How to Keep Getting Extraordinary Things Done in Organizations; James M. Kouzes, Barry Posner, Jossey-Bass, 1995 (Chapters 7 & 8).

Getting Things Done: The Art of Stress-Free Productivity; David Allen, Viking Penguin, 2001.

Delegating Work: Expert Solutions to Everyday Challenges; Harvard Business School Press, 2008.

Self-assessment

 Using the scale provided, rate yourself on the following leadership behaviors.

Poor   Excellent

1   2   3   4   5   6   7

_____ I clearly explain the task I delegate.

_____ I avoid completing the same task I just delegated.

_____ I am available for support and feedback.

_____ I adjust how I follow-up on delegated tasks based on the experience of the person and the requirements of the task.

_____ I use delegation to help me be more time effective.

_____ I use delegation to develop others.

Action Planning Notes

 What three things in this section will help you be a better leader?

1.

2.

3.

What would change if you started or continued doing these three things?

How can you implement these changes?

Dimension 7: Dependability

"Ability is important in our quest for success, but dependability is critical!"

— Zig Ziglar

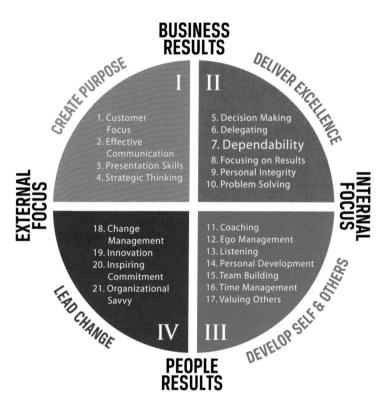

Overview

The leaders who are regarded as dependable are also the ones who understand "execution." These leaders are admired and have reputations for being counted on, for getting things done. They are the ones who, when assigned any task, will come through, and their bosses *know* they will. They are the ones who receive the toughest, most closely watched tasks—the "must do" responsibilities. They have the reputation for doing it—no matter what it takes. What a career asset to have. What a career enhancer for greater opportunities. There are learned behaviors, techniques and practices that can produce this kind of reputation. It does take discipline, hard work, *and* tenacity, but it is "doable", and very worthwhile!

To help you become more dependable, consider the following tips:

Tips

1. Make it your personal creed to complete, on time, every assignment you receive. Exceed the quality standards that were set.

2. The most critical behavior to improve dependability is to make sure you follow through on your commitments.

3. Dependability is largely a perceived concept. Test that perception by soliciting specific feedback from your associates on their view of your dependability and responsibility.

4. Make your word your bond. Do what you say you will.

5. Look out for and suggest new ways to save your organization money. Initiate improvements that align with bigger company goals.

6. Take on and meet additional challenges that the work group faces.

7. Always understand the relationships that your projects

have with others. This will give you a vision of the broader purpose.

8. Develop the habit of doing more than what is expected.

9. Never let down on your level of commitment even though you feel it is not appreciated, you have a disappointing performance review, or you did not receive the bonus you were expecting. Your consistency and attitude will ultimately be recognized. At the very least, you will be true to your own high standards.

10. Be proactive in recognizing what can be done and doing it.

11. Dependability generates trust for you and your work by others. It is essential for long-term success on the job. It demonstrates your commitment and motivation. It underscores your dedication and direct involvement in the organization's future. It develops cooperative and highly productive relationships with others.

12. Be aware of how your piece of a project will accelerate or delay the entire effort.

13. Communication is a hallmark of dependable people. They keep others informed. They keep their boss apprised. They keep their people in the loop of all aspects of important developments.

14. What may seem insignificant to you may be perceived as vital in the eyes of your boss, employees, or peers. Ask others what their priorities are within the project.

15. Discuss with your boss his or her understanding of the characteristics of superior performance. This will help you understand his or her standards.

16. Your reputation is significantly influenced by your dependability and consistency. It will surprise you

how far up and down an organization your reputation will travel. The best long-term self-marketing is to be seen as reliable.

17. Let your own satisfaction be enough to give you the motivation you need to maintain high quality standards of work and job completion. Those who rely on external motivation and "atta-boys" from their boss may not always receive it. Consequently, they may lack the required motivation to get the job done well. Let it come from within.

18. Don't assume that someone else got the message or that a part of the project was completed. Be assertive and follow up to make sure a message was understood.

19. Manage your emotions.

20. Occasionally monitor your personal performance. It is not uncommon for an organization to "raise the bar" of its quality metrics. Stay with or exceed those levels.

21. You are a powerful example to your workgroup or team. The degree to which you are dependable in meeting deadlines and other metrics has significant influence.

22. The most meaningful and critical tasks are usually given to the most reliable and committed people.

23. Be punctual.

24. Develop habitual dependability: make consistency of performance a defining characteristic.

25. Establishing credibility takes consistent effort over time—yet it can be damaged quickly with a single foolish statement or action.

26. Set aside five minutes at the beginning of each day to review your commitments.

27. Stay alert. Keep your antennae fully engaged. Be aware of projects, assignments, steps, phases, and elements that must be done and do them. Solicit feedback

28. Use a notepad or PDA to record action items in meetings.

29. Avoid the practice of committing just to be nice, and then not following through on your commitment.

30. Identify how often you feel overloaded or overwhelmed; this can have a negative effect on your output.

31. Avoid procrastination.

References

The Oz Principle: Getting Results Through Individual and Organizational Accountability; Roger Connors, Tom Smith, Craig Hickman, Prentice Hall, 1994.

The 17 Indisputable Laws of Teamwork; John C. Maxwell, Thomas Nelson Inc., 2001 (see pg. 117-132).

The Ten Commandments of Success; James A. Belasco, New Millennium Press, 2000 (see pg. 97-114).

Getting Things Done: The Art of Stress-Free Productivity; David Allen, Viking Penguin, 2001.

Do It Now!; Andy Bruce and Ken Langdom, DK Publishing Inc., 2001.

Indispensable: How to Become the Company That Your Customers Can't Live Without; Joe Calloway, John Wiley & Sons, Inc., 2005.

Self-assessment

 Using the scale provided, rate yourself on the following leadership behaviors.

Poor 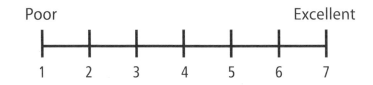 Excellent

1   2   3   4   5   6   7

_____ I consistently meet deadlines.

_____ I consistently meet or exceed expected quality of work.

_____ I know my boss would say that I follow through on my commitments.

_____ I know my direct reports would say that I follow through on my commitments.

_____ I know my peers would say that I follow through on my commitments.

Comments:

Action Planning Notes

 What three things in this section will help you be a better leader?

1.

2.

3.

What would change if you started or continued doing these three things?

How can you implement these changes?

Dimension 8: Focusing on Results

"The greater danger for most of us lies not in setting our aim too high and falling short; but in setting our aim too low, and achieving our mark."

— Michelangelo

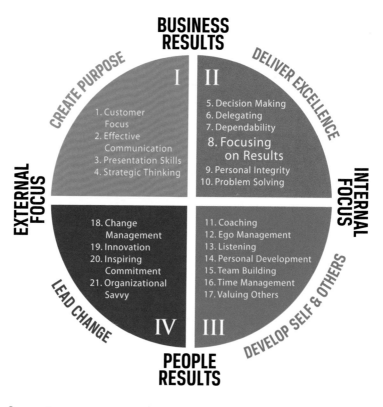

BUSINESS RESULTS

CREATE PURPOSE

DELIVER EXCELLENCE

I
1. Customer Focus
2. Effective Communication
3. Presentation Skills
4. Strategic Thinking

II
5. Decision Making
6. Delegating
7. Dependability
8. Focusing on Results
9. Personal Integrity
10. Problem Solving

EXTERNAL FOCUS

INTERNAL FOCUS

IV
18. Change Management
19. Innovation
20. Inspiring Commitment
21. Organizational Savvy

III
11. Coaching
12. Ego Management
13. Listening
14. Personal Development
15. Team Building
16. Time Management
17. Valuing Others

LEAD CHANGE

DEVELOP SELF & OTHERS

PEOPLE RESULTS

Overview

Today's leaders have very limited time to perform endless requests from key stakeholders *and* the demands of their boss and teams. They must juggle limitless priorities and increasingly complex quantities of work at lower cost, meeting tighter schedules, and coinciding with higher quality standards. Your job is to do it all more efficiently and effectively with the small degree of authority you have, but with all the accountability of a CEO. Achieving desired results requires a huge dose of discipline and focus with continuously improved methods—both personal and professional.

To help you be more effective in focusing on results, consider the following tips:

Tips

1. The key to achieving results is to effectively manage workflow through other people.

2. Refine your delegation skills—this is absolutely crucial! Always try to delegate to the lowest level that you can. It will help them grow and will free your time for other pressing matters. Don't micromanage, but do stay on top of delegated assignments. Be available for support and clarification.

3. Have regular face time with your staff and direct reports to learn how they are doing, what their concerns are, and what you can do to help them meet their objectives.

4. In your interactions with your employees, assess their work loads to determine if tasks are fairly, equally, and wisely distributed given their capabilities and schedules. Involve your people in setting their own performance standards and goals. They will often set higher standards for themselves than you would for them.

5. Be flexible and adaptable in your style so that it meets the individual needs of each of your people. No two are alike, which means that each requires a different approach to maximize their output and commitment.

6. When your people come to you with a problem, have them help you resolve it. They are closest to it, so they are in the best position to recommend the solution or approach.

7. Search and study for quality books and lectures on execution and share the most salient points with your people. Reinforce them through practical application in the workflow.

8. Foster a culture of continuous improvement where everyone takes the initiative to consciously look for ways to enhance processes, systems, and transactions. Demonstrate how everyone wins by increasing quality and decreasing costs. Be alert for problems and respond with a solution.

9. Identify and prioritize the needs of your customer.

10. Keep your boss informed on the progress of your work.

11. Prioritize tasks in order to do quality work while still meeting the schedule.

12. Grow and develop your people. Keep them in a state of readiness for their current and future roles. They will feel challenged and valued because of the essential role they have.

13. Everything has risks. Extreme risk should be avoided, but avoiding all risks should not be an excuse for not moving ahead. Establish mitigators for each risk and move on. Wisely and methodically proceed toward new levels of performance.

14. Carefully review each of your key players. What role and assignment does each have? Judiciously assign the appropriate degree of authority to each one to streamline the workflow.

15. Do not disregard the politics of your environment, but be careful to not let them dominate you, your time, or your attitude.

16. Identify the milestones in each project and focus on achieving them.

17. Remember it's amazing what can be accomplished if you don't care who gets the credit.

18. Create a 30 second elevator speech to explain the business case, and share it with others.

19. Look at the big picture—it helps keep things in perspective.

20. Be careful that you are not holding onto favorite assignments or tasks that bring you personal recognition. These can weigh you down and hold you back.

21. Develop a reputation of dependability by following through on promised items. Be persistent.

22. Focus on results. Don't confuse activity with accomplishments. Work smarter, not harder. Long hours and lists of "to-dos" don't always equate to effective performance.

23. Stay healthy. Keep your energy level high and steady—others will feel your energy.

24. Frequently review your progress relative to your goals and targets.

25. Use tested and proven metrics to measure all aspects of the workflow.

26. Remember the higher up you go, the more you need others to help get the work done. Beware of being perceived as trying to get ahead at the expense of others. You could become the victim of sabotage. Eagerly share credit and include others.

27. Always provide closure to your boss, customers, and people.

28. Ask, "How can I/we add value to _____?" Then follow through.

29. Remove obstacles to help your group achieve their goals.

30. Beware of complaining. It will label you as being negative. Avoid negative talk, but don't ignore reality checks.

31. Keep goals visible and review daily.

32. Identify who can kill the project or idea and make sure they are onboard.

33. Demonstrate your orientation to action through careful risk-taking, exceeding performance targets, and going beyond the expected.

34. Identify the risks to the project based on impact (high/low) and probability (high/low).

35. Celebrate achievement and accomplishment.

36. Identify critical paths and remove impeding obstacles.

37. Remember a "B" plan executed in an "A" fashion is better than an "A" plan executed in a "B" fashion.

38. Never forget the importance of *what* you are doing and *who* you are doing it for.

39. Make it happen.

References

Sacred Cows Make the Best Burgers: Developing Change-Ready People and Organizations; Robert Kriegel, David Brandt, Warner, 1996.

The Seven Habits of Highly Effective People; Stephen R. Covey, Simon & Schuster, 1989.

The Performance Edge: New Strategies to Maximize Your Work Effectiveness and Competitive Advantage; Robert Cooper, Houghton Mifflin, 1991.

How to Be a Star at Work: Nine Breakthrough Strategies You Need to Succeed; Robert E. Kelley, Times Business-Random House, 1999.

Good to Great: Why Some Companies Make the Leap . . . and Others Don't; Jim Collins, Harper Collins, 2001.

Getting Things Done: The Art of Stress-Free Productivity; David Allen, Viking Penguin, 2001.

Execution: The Discipline of Getting Things Done; Larry Bossidy, Ram Charan, Crown Publishing Group, 2002.

Managing the Unexpected: Assuring High Performance in an Age of Complexity; Karl Weick, Jossey-Bass, 2001.

What the CEO Wants You to Know; Ram Charan, Crown Business Books, 2001.

The Carrot Principle; Adrian Gostick, Chester Elton, Free Press, 2009.

The First 90 Days: Critical Success Strategies for New Leaders at All Levels; Michael Watkins, Harvard Business School Press, 2003.

Self-assessment

 Using the scale provided, rate yourself on the following leadership behaviors.

Poor   Excellent

1   2   3   4   5   6   7

_____ I start with the end in mind.

_____ I remain focused during stressful situations.

_____ I establish clear measures to monitor and measure performance.

_____ I establish clear and realistic timelines.

_____ I establish agreed upon roles and responsibilities.

_____ I establish agreed upon deliverables.

_____ I hold others accountable.

_____ I hold myself accountable.

Comments:

Action Planning Notes

What three things in this section will help you be a better leader?

1.

2.

3.

What would change if you started or continued doing these three things?

How can you implement these changes?

Dimension 9: Personal Integrity

"What lies behind us and what lies before us are tiny matters compared to what lies within us."

— Ralph Waldo Emerson

BUSINESS RESULTS

CREATE PURPOSE

DELIVER EXCELLENCE

I

II

1. Customer Focus
2. Effective Communication
3. Presentation Skills
4. Strategic Thinking

5. Decision Making
6. Delegating
7. Dependability
8. Focusing on Results
9. Personal Integrity
10. Problem Solving

EXTERNAL FOCUS

INTERNAL FOCUS

18. Change Management
19. Innovation
20. Inspiring Commitment
21. Organizational Savvy

11. Coaching
12. Ego Management
13. Listening
14. Personal Development
15. Team Building
16. Time Management
17. Valuing Others

LEAD CHANGE

DEVELOP SELF & OTHERS

IV

III

PEOPLE RESULTS

Overview

The single most important attribute that a leader can have is to be trusted by others. If this trust is gone, then all else is moot. Trust must be earned over time—with consistent actions, words and intentions. Trust cannot be demanded or expected. One careless or thoughtless act can hinder or even destroy it. The essence of trust is integrity. Over the course of your career, you will likely have the opportunity to face compromising situations. How you handle these will directly impact your reputation and—more importantly—how you view yourself. The result will be how others view you, your credibility, and the future trust that your associates have for you. The basic premise is knowing your values and having the moral courage to live true to them.

To help you be more effective in personal integrity, consider the following tips:

Tips

1. Ask yourself these questions if you are ever in a quandary over a tough ethical dilemma:
   - Am I hurting the reputation of another?
   - Will I destroy the trust I have tried so hard to establish?
   - What would my mother say?
   - If this became front-page material in the newspaper, how would I feel?
   - Is it fair to all parties?
   - How will I feel about myself?
   - How would I explain my actions to my family?
   - Does it promote a win-win relationship?

2. Be careful when making promises. People remember these and will hold you to them. Only make promises if you truly plan (and are able) to keep them. Keep track of any promises and commitments (implied or direct) that you make. Monitor them. Your follow-

through will directly influence other's trust in your future promises and commitments.

3. Your behavior best models your true ethical beliefs.

4. Does your organization have a written code of values or ethics? If so, find it, read it, learn it, and be true to it. Teach it to others. Become a living example of it to your associates. Model it in all your transactions. Encourage others to do the same. If your organization does not have a code of values, start one.

5. When you make a mistake, admit it. Everyone will make a poor choice or wrong decision. Few will acknowledge doing so. People will admire your honesty. They will also be more likely to follow your example.

6. The world is so small that if you choose to burn bridges it is very likely that you will be forced to rebuild them in the future.

7. Ask trusted associates their opinion of your trustworthiness and honesty. Listen openly to them without rationalizing.

8. Inaction on your part in addressing an unethical situation can create the impression that you and your department or organization condone such behavior.

9. Keep in mind a modified golden rule: "Do unto others what you hope they would do unto you."

10. Encourage open and honest discussions about ethical issues as they surface.

11. Try using this rule of thumb when confronted with a tough ethical dilemma: "If someone else came to you with this situation, what counsel would you give them?"

12. Building a reputation of trust takes time. It is an ongoing process. It is not based on a single event or moment. It is influenced by a series of interactions, behaviors, and experiences—all observed by others who formulate the perception of trust and honesty over time.

13. Establish the norm of frank, honest, and open communication with employees, customers, vendors, and all stakeholders. This will directly contribute to an environment of trust.

14. Make sure there is consistency between your words and your actions.

15. Create an environment where people are comfortable coming to you with their concerns. HONOR THEIR CONFIDENCE. The trust and confidence of your people and your superiors is absolutely essential for you to succeed!

16. Your people will be less willing to share information with you if you are not trusted. This will hurt your effectiveness because you will undoubtedly miss out on vital and necessary confidential information that you need to know.

17. Resist making commitments to others just to placate them. If you do, and you don't stand true to them, your reputation and integrity will be damaged.

18. Trust is *everything*! It doesn't matter how brilliant, competent, talented, or skilled a person is. If their trustworthiness is questionable, all performance is in serious jeopardy.

19. Seek advice from your firm's ethics officer or ombudsman.

20. Unintended promises and commitments can be read into your statements. Use clear and unambiguous wording to avoid confusion.

21. When challenged or questioned, give straightforward, complete, and honest answers. Evasive replies will catch up to you and damage your credibility and integrity.

22. Don't withhold information that your team needs. Keep them current and fully informed.

23. Lead by example—take the 1st, 2nd, and 3rd bullets to protect your team.

24. Be careful about being too anxious to make the sale—you are likely to over-promise.

25. Be true to your word.

References

Integrity; Stephen L. Carter, Harper Perennial, 1996.

The Power of Ethical Management: Integrity Pays; Ken Blanchard, Norman Vincent Peale, Morrow, 1988.

Solving Costly Organizational Conflict; Robert Blake, Jane Mouton, Jossey-Bass, 1984.

The Leadership Challenge: How to Keep Getting Extraordinary Things Done in Organizations; James M. Kouzes, Barry Posner, Jossey-Bass, 1995 (Chapters 7-9).

Survival of the Savvy: High-Integrity Political Tactics for Career and Company Success; Rick Brandon, Marty Seldman, Simon & Schuster Adult Publishing Group, 2004.

High Performance with High Integrity; Ben W. Heineman, Harvard Business School Press, 2008.

Integrity: The Courage to Meet the Demands of Reality; Henry Cloud, Collins Business, 2006.

Winners Never Cheat; John Huntsman, Wharton University Press, 2005.

The Speed of Trust; Stephen M.R. Covey, Free Press, 2008.

Self-assessment

 Using the scale provided, rate yourself on the following leadership behaviors.

Poor   Excellent

1   2   3   4   5   6   7

_____ I do what I say.

_____ I consider ethical implications before making a business decision.

_____ I privately support issues/decisions I support in public.

_____ I advise others to remain true to their values.

_____ I model the values of the organization.

Action Planning Notes

 What three things in this section will help you be a better leader?

1.

2.

3.

What would change if you started or continued doing these three things?

How can you implement these changes?

Dimension 10: Problem Solving

"The significant problems we have cannot be solved at the same level of thinking with which we created them."

— Albert Einstein

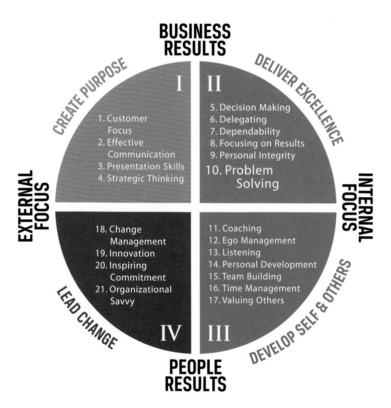

BUSINESS RESULTS

CREATE PURPOSE

DELIVER EXCELLENCE

I

1. Customer Focus
2. Effective Communication
3. Presentation Skills
4. Strategic Thinking

II

5. Decision Making
6. Delegating
7. Dependability
8. Focusing on Results
9. Personal Integrity
10. Problem Solving

EXTERNAL FOCUS

INTERNAL FOCUS

IV

18. Change Management
19. Innovation
20. Inspiring Commitment
21. Organizational Savvy

III

11. Coaching
12. Ego Management
13. Listening
14. Personal Development
15. Team Building
16. Time Management
17. Valuing Others

LEAD CHANGE

DEVELOP SELF & OTHERS

PEOPLE RESULTS

Overview

As a leader, one of your primary objectives is to identify and address obstacles and roadblocks that impede your team's ability to accomplish their objectives and reach their targets. This is done through effective and creative problem solving. Resolving these challenges requires ingenuity and creativity so that the work you are responsible for continues within the allotted schedule and budget. To do this often necessitates that you use the limits of your authority, all available resources, your network of professionals, and every other avenue you can imagine. Resolving problems is likely one of the most difficult aspects of a leader's job description. It is never easy.

To help you be more effective in problem solving, consider the following tips (also see the tips in the "Decision Making" section—many of them also apply to problem solving):

Tips

1. Be careful that the problem you have identified is not really a symptom. Focus on the core issue, not its effects. The first and most critical step in problem solving is accurately defining the problem. Peter Drucker's statement is on target: "A problem well defined is a problem half-solved." Accurately defining a problem will take a while, so be patient and persistent. Test it. Question it. Validate it.

2. As you begin the process, ask each team member to state the problem as *they* see it—in their own words. This step will ensure that you look at the problem from multiple perspectives.

3. Write the problem definition on a white board or flip chart so that all can see it during the problem-solving process.

4. Have your team look at the history of the problem. Review how it has been dealt with in the past. Consider the culture and norms that have shaped the current situation.

5. List all related aspects of the problem by topics: symptoms, ancillary, directly related to, result of, etc. This will help you sort out "relevant causes."

6. Optimal size of a brainstorming, problem solving group is 5-8 people of varied backgrounds. Brainstorming is only effective when the #1 rule of brainstorming is not violated. The rule is that there is to be no criticism or evaluation (verbal or nonverbal) of any suggestion that is brought forward. An atmosphere of "anything goes" must be established. Then, once the brainstorming session ends, the critiquing begins.

7. In determining potential answers or solutions, don't ignore gut instinct, hunches, feelings, and unexpected or illogical ideas. Keep a separate list of these. They often pay off in some way and to some degree.

8. Use all available tools, forms, data, metrics, and official or unofficial input to help identify causes and possible solutions. Don't overlook or ignore anything.

9. A very worthwhile problem-solving technique is the Janusian approach (named for the Roman god of beginnings and endings—Janus, whose head appears on both sides of Roman coins). You merely ask two sets of questions:

Set 1:
- Who is most likely to respond to this situation?
- How has the situation been addressed in the past?

- Which tools and processes have been used to address similar problems?

Set 2 asks the opposite:

- Who is *least* likely to respond to this situation?
- How has this situation NOT been addressed in the past?
- Which tools and processes have NOT been used to address similar problems?

You will be amazed at how limiting your approach has been using Set 1 questions, and how mind-expanding Set 2 questions enable you to be.

10. Place your problem in a new or different context. Seek to relate it to another setting, one that might help you see it in a different light.

11. Does current pressure from budgets, schedules, senior management, media, etc. limit or restrict your vision of the real cause(s) of your problem? Imagine a situation where you are free of these pressures. How would you then see your problem, issue, or concern?

12. A key piece of the process, which is too often overlooked, is the *implementation of the solution phase*. You must examine: 1) the available resources for implementation; 2) who will be impacted; 3) potential resistance to the solution and why; 4) communication and explanation of the solution; and 5) all additional impacts.

13. Make sure your problem-solving team has a balance of logical thinkers and creative thinkers. You need *both*!

You also need differing backgrounds, knowledge, and expertise to bring out the varied perspectives and views that are required to successfully solve problems.

14. One approach is to share the problem with someone who has no part in the process. They will look at it with complete objectivity and a fresh perspective. Then share their input with the rest of the team.

15. Make sure that while searching for causes and solutions, all ideas are completely clarified. Too often, suggested thoughts are not heard clearly, are misunderstood, or are heard through biased filters. Consequently, these ideas are dismissed. Seek clarification. Ask questions of the contributor. It is enlightening to the team to see what emerges as a result of this clarification.

16. The beginnings of some of the best solutions often come from the least likely sources. Be sure you seek input from young or inexperienced members of your team as well as from seasoned leaders.

17. Identify what your customer values.

18. Avoid jumping to conclusions too early.

19. Two approaches to problem solving:

    • Convergent—a logical and deliberate, defined path leading toward a solution.
    • Divergent—a more creative approach relying on intuition, humor, absurdity, and innovation.

20. The first step to creative problem solving is thinking outside the norm. Avoid boxed-in thinking and mental ruts brought on by closed-minded rigidity.

21. How you handle the "little things" will often prevent

them from becoming "big" problems to be solved down the road.

22. Do not define a problem with an inherent solution.

23. Beware of the stories we tell ourselves in our heads—they are often exaggerated and not accurate.

24. Avoid forcing a solution into pre-existing conditions.

25. The typical steps in a problem-solving cycle include:

    1. Defining the problem
    2. Generating solutions
    3. Selecting a solution
    4. Implementing the solution
    5. Evaluating the implementation
    6. Improving continuously

References

Breakthrough Thinking: Why We Must Change the Way We Solve Problems, and the Seven Principles to Achieve This; Gerald Nadler, Shozo Hibino, Prima Publishing, 1990.

That's No Problem!: A Problem-free Approach to Problem Solving; Dr. Marlene Caroselli, AMI How-To Series, American Media Publishing, 1997.

Conflict In Organizations: Practical Solutions Any Manager Can Use; S. Turner, F. Weed, Prentice-Hall, 1983.

Managing Conflict: Interpersonal Dialogue and Third Party Roles; Richard Watton, Addison-Wesley, 1987.

Effective Group Problem Solving; William M. Fox, Jossey-Bass, 1987.

Getting Things Done: The Art of Stress-Free Productivity;

David Allen, Viking Penguin, 2001.

101 Creative Problem Solving Techniques: The Handbook of New Ideas for Business; James M. Higgins, New Management Publishing Co., 2006.

The Thinker's Toolkit: 14 Powerful Techniques for Problem Solving; Morgan D. Jones, Three Rivers Press, 1998.

Getting to Yes: Negotiating Agreement Without Giving In; Roger Fisher, Bruce M. Patton, William L. Ury, Houghton Mifflin, 1992.

Common Sense Management: Quick Wisdom for Good Managers; Roger Fulton, Ten Speed Press, 2009.

Self-assessment

 Using the scale provided, rate yourself on the following leadership behaviors.

_____ I clearly identify and define a problem.

_____ I obtain multiple perspectives when identifying a problem.

_____ I look to see how others have addressed a similar problem.

_____ I consider multiple methods on how to solve a problem.

_____ I effectively prioritize problems.

_____ I effectively manage people in addressing problems.

_____ I continuously seek to improve a solution.

Comments:

Action Planning Notes

 What three things in this section will help you be a better leader?

1.

2.

3.

What would change if you started or continued doing these three things?

How can you implement these changes?

Dimension 11: Coaching

"A bit of fragrance always clings to the hand that gives you roses."

— Chinese Proverb

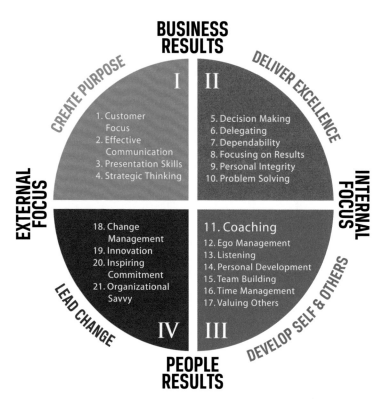

BUSINESS RESULTS

CREATE PURPOSE

DELIVER EXCELLENCE

I

1. Customer Focus
2. Effective Communication
3. Presentation Skills
4. Strategic Thinking

II

5. Decision Making
6. Delegating
7. Dependability
8. Focusing on Results
9. Personal Integrity
10. Problem Solving

EXTERNAL FOCUS

INTERNAL FOCUS

IV

18. Change Management
19. Innovation
20. Inspiring Commitment
21. Organizational Savvy

III

11. Coaching
12. Ego Management
13. Listening
14. Personal Development
15. Team Building
16. Time Management
17. Valuing Others

LEAD CHANGE

DEVELOP SELF & OTHERS

PEOPLE RESULTS

Overview

One of the primary jobs you have is developing your people. You are responsible and accountable to both your employees and the organization to train and grow your people so that they can perform at their full potential. This necessitates a conscious desire and awareness on your part to invest your time in their growth. No two people are alike. Each will require a tailored approach, which necessitates flexibility on your part. This requires that you learn effective coaching skills.

To help you be more effective in coaching, consider the following tips, organized by General Tips, Career Coaching Tips, and Corrective Coaching Tips:

Tips

General Tips

1. Care must be taken to establish a positive, comfortable, and compatible environment between the employee and the coach.

2. Determine the person's motivational level to decide the best approach.

3. For supervisors and managers, a major focus area is often improving their interpersonal skills.

4. Provide 360 assessment or feedback counseling for higher-level performers to help them learn of their strengths and deficiencies. Help them build on their strengths and improve or compensate for their weaknesses.

5. Focus on the behavior, not your perception or interpretation of the behavior.

6. Take advantage of coachable moments.

7. Provide specific and frequent performance feedback.

8. Challenge others to do more.

9. You don't need to win every battle to win the war.

10. Give people options and choices—it is empowering.

11. Coaching attributes and roles include:

- Being a good listener
- Giving feedback
- Being supportive
- Offering suggestions
- Providing appropriate praise
- Holding others accountable
- Being patient
- Giving regular performance reviews
- Explaining the "why"
- Being open-minded
- Following up
- Teaching
- Being the example

Career Coaching Tips

12. In career coaching, encourage the positive performer to spend time learning more about the description, actual job duties, and responsibilities of future desirable positions.

13. Career coaching done effectively plays a major role in succession planning. It directly strengthens your organization's bench strength.

14. Tailor career coaching to mesh with the person's career goals and potential.

15. Career coaching provides emotional support and encouragement to try things people normally would not try. This is especially worthwhile when they have shown greater potential or propensities toward a par-

ticular area.

Corrective Coaching Tips

16. Coaching is only employed when you believe the deficiency is correctable, the person has the capacity to do the work properly, and the person wants to improve.

17. Addressing poor or unacceptable performance must be done right away. It cannot be procrastinated.

18. Don't spend so much time coaching low performers that your star performers feel neglected.

19. Simple corrective feedback should be tried before formal coaching is started.

20. On-the-job-training (OJT) and coaching may be delegated and do not always require the direct supervisor. Feel free to seek a second opinion from HR or a trusted associate.

21. Allow them appropriate and reasonable time to settle into a new position. This will be shorter for hourly, skilled workers and longer for management positions.

22. For senior managers who are obviously deficient in an area they cannot remedy consider adding a person to the team with a strength that will compensate.

23. Remember the easiest way to strip someone's dignity is to reprimand him or her publicly.

24. You must be specific in letting others know exactly what they did and why it is unacceptable.

25. Separate the person from the act. Condemn the action, but reinforce the person.

26. Remind them of how much you value them.

27. Ask them what specifically they can do to avoid repeating the behavior in the future.

28. Be available to them for future help.

29. Don't keep reminding them of their mistakes or short-comings.

30. Draw out from those being coached what their opinion is of why their work or skill levels are weak. Then probe for causes and reasons.

31. Help them learn and master proper methods that will result in meeting desired outcomes.

32. Have follow-up meetings to monitor results. Hold them accountable once performance standards are made clear.

33. Document, as needed, all discussions for future reference.

References

The Heart of Coaching; Thomas Crane, F T A Press, 2007.

Masterful Coaching; Robert Hargrove, Pfeiffer, 2008.

Coaching for Leadership; Marshall Goldsmith, Laurance Lyons, Pfeiffer, 2005.

Goal Setting: A Motivational Technique That Works!; Edwin A. Locke, Gary Latham, 1984.

Please Understand Me: Character and Temperament Types; David Keirsey, Marilyn Bates, Prometheus Nemesis, 1984.

The Empowered Manager: Positive Political Skills At Work; Peter Block, Jossey-Bass, 1990.

Putting the One Minute Manager to Work: How to Turn the 3 Secrets Into Skills; Ken Blanchard, Robert Larker, Morrow & Company, 1984.

The Art and Practice of Leadership Coaching; Howard Morgan, Phil Hawkins, Marshall Goldsmith, John Wiley & Sons, 2005.

Executive Coaching; Peter Stephenson, Prentice Hall, 2000.

Talent is Overrated: What Really Separates World-class Performers from Everybody Else; Geoff Colvin, Penguin Books, 2008.

Now, Discover Your Strengths; Marcus Buckingham, Donald Clifton, Free Press, 2001.

The Rules of Work; Richard Templar, Prentice Hall Business, 2003.

Strengths-Based Leadership; Tom Rath, Barry Conchie, Gallup Press, 2008.

Self-assessment

 Using the scale provided, rate yourself on the following leadership behaviors.

Poor   Excellent

1   2   3   4   5   6   7

_____ I am an effective coach in helping employees improve their performance.

_____ I give feedback specifically, professionally, and in a timely manner.

_____ I make certain that people receive necessary and timely training and development.

_____ I help employees develop, recognize, and appreciate a strong sense of personal accomplishment.

_____ I have a flexible management style for a variety of challenges and people.

Comments:

Action Planning Notes

 What three things in this section will help you be a better leader?

1.

2.

3.

What would change if you started or continued doing these three things?

How can you implement these changes?

Dimension 12: Ego Management

"Of all manifestations of power, restraint impresses men the most."

— Thucydides

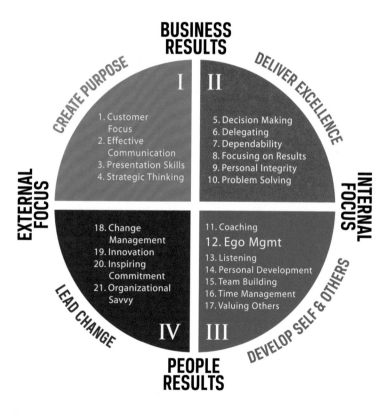

BUSINESS RESULTS

CREATE PURPOSE

DELIVER EXCELLENCE

I

1. Customer Focus
2. Effective Communication
3. Presentation Skills
4. Strategic Thinking

II

5. Decision Making
6. Delegating
7. Dependability
8. Focusing on Results
9. Personal Integrity
10. Problem Solving

EXTERNAL FOCUS

INTERNAL FOCUS

IV

18. Change Management
19. Innovation
20. Inspiring Commitment
21. Organizational Savvy

III

11. Coaching
12. Ego Mgmt
13. Listening
14. Personal Development
15. Team Building
16. Time Management
17. Valuing Others

LEAD CHANGE

DEVELOP SELF & OTHERS

PEOPLE RESULTS

Overview

People need a strong ego to handle all that life throws at them. The challenge is to manage the ego so it doesn't manage you! A balanced ego guards against excessive human pride and vanity. It embodies the right balance of humility and modesty with strong inner conviction and determination. Truly successful leaders learn to balance their egos. They share the spotlight. They lead the applause for their people. They don't care who gets the credit—what is important is getting the job done.

To help you be more effective in managing your ego, consider the following tips (also see the tips in the "Listening" section—many of them apply to ego management):

Tips

1. Caution is required in times of stress and pressure. This is the time, unfortunately, when the ugly part of the ego can break loose and control your interaction with others—usually causing regret later on.

2. People with excessive egos receive less feedback, which prevents growth opportunities. People are not as comfortable or willing to approach those who have overly strong egos.

3. Don't take yourself too seriously. Laugh more.

4. Successful ego management allows you to become more flexible in a variety of ways. This is a real asset to your effectiveness and leadership.

5. Observe others in your organization, especially senior managers and executives. Notice the way they manage their egos (either poorly or well). Then study how others react to them because of this.

6. Poorly managed egos can lead to regrettable and disruptive behavior.

7. Dominant egos may result in others feeling inadequate

or inferior.

8. Inflated egos frequently end up in unproductive (and even destructive) gamesmanship sessions where no one wins.

9. It is difficult to be sensitive to the challenges that coworkers and teammates have when the leader is all wrapped up in him or herself.

10. Good ego management is influenced by the degree to which you have compassion for others. You "feel" for others who are struggling with an assignment or challenge, and consequently, offer help or advice.

11. Resilience, the ability to "bounce back," is another characteristic of a healthy ego. Following a major disappointment or defeat, the well-balanced ego (more humble now) learns from the experience and tries again.

12. Be empathetic to others when appropriate. Demonstrate your concern for them with a brief conversation.

13. In problem-solving settings, don't be the first to offer an opinion. Let others do so. Recognize and acknowledge their input. Point out the merits of their contribution. As you express your views be careful not to make your ideas (verbally or nonverbally) the only right answer.

14. Slow your reaction time; reflect before deciding.

15. Ask yourself, "Will how I handle this issue negatively affect important relationships?"

16. No one has a monopoly on truth. A well-managed ego knows this and welcomes participation from others.

17. Support decisions others come up with, even when they don't coincide with yours.

18. Be attentive to others as you listen and converse. Don't dominate the conversation. Engage others. Encourage the sharing of their thoughts.

19. Demonstrate patience with others who are wrestling with a new assignment. Coach them as needed.

20. Be open to considering other's inputs—not just in a token manner, which can be perceived as patronizing —especially if you are very good at doing that same assignment.

21. A sign of a healthy ego is the degree to which you are adaptable to change. Ego-driven people want the world to conform to them. Well-managed egos adapt to new rules, norms, and requirements.

22. Having an "inflated ego" is often more perception than reality. The best starting point is to improve your listening skills.

23. Learn to ask, "What do you think?" more often. Involve people in your thinking. It will make them feel of greater value while decreasing their perception that you have an over-inflated ego.

24. Test yourself on how you respond to others. Do you listen to their input? Do you acknowledge their suggestions?

25. Manage your own conversational tangents. Keep them under control.

26. Be genuinely courteous to others.

27. Do not burn bridges. You might have to cross them in the future.

28. Learn to control your temper.

29. Don't favor certain people with your time.

30. Pay attention to how much "talk time" you take in meetings and decrease it as necessary.

31. Tame your tongue.

32. Admit mistakes. You will then show others, by your example, to do the same.

33. Think what is best for the team—not just for yourself.

34. Recognize that even if you are right, you can't be successful without other people's involvement and ideas.

35. Treat others as equal partners.

36. Share positive feedback with others on a regular basis. Share the credit. Share the spotlight. Lead the applause for others.

37. Avoid sarcasm and putdowns in public and private.

38. Ask for formal feedback from others (360 assessment, interviews, etc.). When you receive it, analyze it, and consider it, without rationalizing.

References

Egonomics: What Makes Ego Our Greatest Asset (or Most Expensive Liability); David Marcum, Steven Smith, Fireside, 2008.

People Skills; Robert Bolton, Touchstone Books, 1986.

Messages: The Communication Skills Book; Matthew McKay, Martha Davis, Patrick Fanning, New Harbinger, 1983.

Forgive and Forget; Lewis B. Smedes, Pocket Books, 1988.

The Seven Habits of Highly Effective People; Stephen R.

Covey, Simon & Schuster, 1989.

Listen Up! Hear What's Really Being Said; Jim Dugger, AMI How-To Series, American Media Publishing, 1995.

Mine's Bigger Than Yours: Understanding and Handling Egos at Work; Susan Debnam, Cyan Communications, 2006.

Why CEOs Fail; David Dotlich, Peter Cairo, Jossey-Bass, 2003.

Now, Discover Your Strengths; Marcus Buckingham, Donald Clifton, Free Press, 2001.

Self-assessment

 Using the scale provided, rate yourself on the following leadership behaviors.

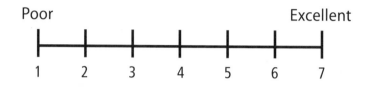

Poor   Excellent

1   2   3   4   5   6   7

_____ I ask others, "What do you think?"

_____ I compliment others on their efforts and accomplishments.

_____ I give credit where credit is due.

_____ I treat others as equals.

_____ I don't dominate conversations.

_____ I share the spotlight.

_____ I ask for feedback and welcome it.

Comments:

Action Planning Notes

What three things in this section will help you be a better leader?

1.

2.

3.

What would change if you started or continued doing these three things?

How can you implement these changes?

Dimension 13: Listening

"The courage to speak must be matched by the wisdom
to listen."

— Anonymous

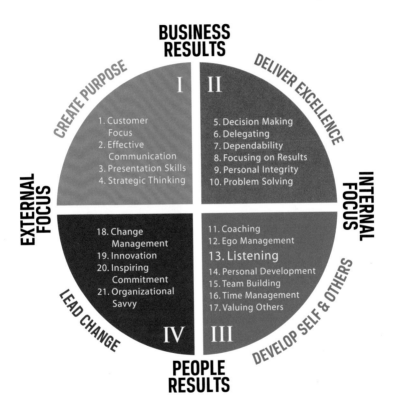

BUSINESS RESULTS

CREATE PURPOSE

DELIVER EXCELLENCE

I

1. Customer Focus
2. Effective Communication
3. Presentation Skills
4. Strategic Thinking

II

5. Decision Making
6. Delegating
7. Dependability
8. Focusing on Results
9. Personal Integrity
10. Problem Solving

EXTERNAL FOCUS

INTERNAL FOCUS

18. Change Management
19. Innovation
20. Inspiring Commitment
21. Organizational Savvy

11. Coaching
12. Ego Management
13. Listening
14. Personal Development
15. Team Building
16. Time Management
17. Valuing Others

LEAD CHANGE

DEVELOP SELF & OTHERS

IV

III

PEOPLE RESULTS

Overview

Listening is a critical skill that underlies all of leadership and management. It can also be the most underestimated and neglected. In many professional assessments it is, unfortunately, the one area in which many leaders receive the lowest evaluations form their direct reports and other associates. Successful listening sends an undeniable message to others that you care about them, their ideas, and their contribution to the organization. Good listening skills directly affect problem solving, decision making and maintaining good working relationships.

To help you be more effective as a listener, consider the following tips (also see the tips in the "Ego Management" section—many of them apply to listening):

Tips

1. Listen without judgment.

2. Try to identify a person's intent as you listen. What is he or she really trying to say?

3. Are the nonverbal signals consistent with the words? If not, focus on the nonverbal signals.

4. Be empathetic to others as you listen. Place yourself in their shoes. Where are they coming from and what is really behind their concerns?

5. Be aware of your own filters (emotions, biases, assumptions).

6. Ask for clarification to make sure you have interpreted correctly what was said.

7. The better listener you are, the more control you can have of the situation.

8. Regular one-on-one listening to each person you manage will reap very positive results for you *and* for them.

9. Reflective listening will help your people solve their own challenges. It will prevent you from dictating a

solution that they may not support.

10. When you talk to others one-on-one, remove physical barriers—don't sit behind your desk or workstation.

11. Listening with genuine intent lets others know you truly care about them and their concerns.

12. During brainstorming sessions, make sure others do more talking than you do.

13. Send positive body language signals. Avoid nonverbal cues that may cause them to think you have tuned them out.

14. Listening to your boss takes on a unique set of parameters. Try to identify his or her agenda, hot buttons, stresses, concerns, and objectives. This will help you place in better context what he or she is saying. It will also help you understand how and when to respond.

15. Never hesitate to seek clarification. This will let the speaker know you are sincere in wanting to understand.

16. Learn to know and recognize the filter (biases, emotions, prejudices, assumptions) of your boss, each of your employees, and peers. This will minimize misunderstanding them, and further help you identify your own filters.

17. Attentive listening in times of conflict is particularly important. These critical moments require that you be tuned into every cue, signal, nuance, gesture, hesitation, and emotion. Watch their faces and eyes, listen for tone and pitch changes, study inflections and reactions.

18. Folded arms can often signal being tuned out. Restless

motions can indicate boredom. Eyes looking to the side may signal that your attention is being drawn away by something or someone else. Tapping a pen denotes nervousness. These and other nonverbal cues can be very revealing. Pick up on them.

19. When you listen, seek clarification by asking questions and paraphrasing back.

20. Remember: people don't care how much you know until they know how much you care. Listening effectively is the best way to let others know you care.

21. Refrain from automatically solving the person's problem. Often they just need to be heard.

22. Avoid being critical and judgmental, which can often increase emotions or turn people off.

23. Good listening skills help you:
    - Hear more accurately.
    - Respond to what you hear.
    - Learn more.
    - Understand more of what you hear.
    - Remember more of what you hear.

24. Listen with your ears AND your eyes.

25. Communication is 20 percent verbal (requiring your ears) and 80 percent nonverbal (requiring your eyes). (Nonverbal includes posture, eyes, tone, face, body, intensity, energy, clothing, atmosphere, furniture, mood, etc.)

26. Attributes of a Good Listener:
    - Search for common ground.
    - Keep an open mind.
    - Be interested and attentive.

- Don't give advice.
- Give nonverbal acknowledgments (head nod, eye contact, facial expression, smile).

27. Resist distractions (digital devices, cell phones, etc.). Keep your focus on the person you are listening to.

28. Control and manage your ego.

29. Clear your mind of distractions prior to engaging in the conversation.

30. Listen to understand, not to respond. Don't form rebuttals while the other person is speaking. Additionally, remain silent when appropriate—don't interrupt.

31. Ask open-ended clarifying questions (e.g., what do you mean, why do you feel that way, why do you say that, could you elaborate on that, how so, what happened next, what I hear you saying is, how do you feel about that, etc.) to get a realistic and accurate understanding of the issues under consideration. These phrases reinforce to other people that you are truly listening.

References

Listening Behavior; Larry Barker, Prentice-Hall, 1971.

How to Speak. How to Listen; M.J. Adler, Collier, 1983.

Listening: The Forgotten Skill; Madelyn Burley-Allen, John Wiley & Sons, 1995.

I Hear You: Listening to Make You a Better Manager; W.E. Atwater, Prentice-Hall, 1982.

Are You Really Listening?: Keys to Successful Communication;

Paul J. Donoghue, Mary E. Siegel, Sorin Book, 2005.

Listen Up!: Hear What's Really Being Said; Jim Dugger, AMI How-To Series, American Media Publishing, 1995.

The 7 Powers of Questions: Secrets to Successful Communication in Life and at Work; Dorothy Leeds, Perigee Trade, 2000.

Self-assessment

 Using the scale provided, rate yourself on the following leadership behaviors.

Poor   Excellent

1   2   3   4   5   6   7

_____ I suspend judgment when listening to others.

_____ I keep eye contact with others when listening.

_____ I pay attention to their nonverbals.

_____ I ask questions without having pre-determined solutions.

_____ I rephrase comments to ensure understanding.

Comments:

Action Planning Notes

What three things in this section will help you be a better leader?

1.

2.

3.

What would change if you started or continued doing these three things?

How can you implement these changes?

Dimension 14: Personal Development

"The unexamined life is not worth living."
— Socrates

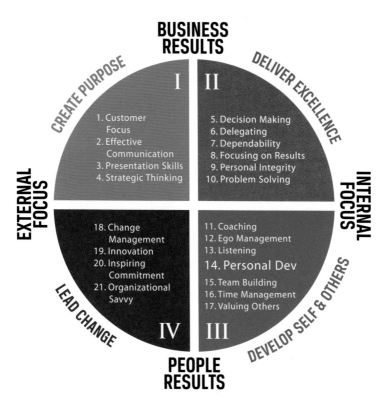

BUSINESS RESULTS

CREATE PURPOSE

I

1. Customer Focus
2. Effective Communication
3. Presentation Skills
4. Strategic Thinking

DELIVER EXCELLENCE

II

5. Decision Making
6. Delegating
7. Dependability
8. Focusing on Results
9. Personal Integrity
10. Problem Solving

EXTERNAL FOCUS

INTERNAL FOCUS

IV

18. Change Management
19. Innovation
20. Inspiring Commitment
21. Organizational Savvy

LEAD CHANGE

III

11. Coaching
12. Ego Management
13. Listening
14. Personal Dev
15. Team Building
16. Time Management
17. Valuing Others

DEVELOP SELF & OTHERS

PEOPLE RESULTS

Overview

The wise Socratic injunction "know thyself" is applicable for all professionals at every stage of their careers. The more we are aware of 1) our talents *and* 2) our behaviors that impair our performance, the more effective we will be in all aspects of our work and lives. Self-awareness is the first step in developing ourselves. Always have the attitude of wanting to improve.

To help you be more effective in your personal development, consider the following tips:

Tips

1. Identify your strengths and build on them.

2. Four areas to focus on in developing yourself:
   - Effectiveness in handling conflict
   - Ability to manage one's ego
   - Capability to see and understand situations through the eyes of *others*
   - Frequency and degree of anger

3. You are in charge of making sure self-development results from your experiences. Turn them into learning modules.

4. Self-development is a never-ending process. It starts with acceptance of personal awareness and continues through with determination to improve.

5. Be aware of "time robbers" that subtly steal your time that otherwise could be spent building and improving your personal development "tool kit." Utilize small moments each day to ponder and analyze growth opportunities.

6. Assess your current capabilities. Identify where you would like to be in five years. What will that require? Now define the gap between where you are and where you would like to be. This becomes your starting point for your personal development.

7. Be open to feedback about your own performance.

8. Review listening tips and improve your active listening skills.

9. Take advantage of personal feedback from assessments (360, performance reviews, etc.) to let you see yourself through the eyes of others. When you receive it, be careful not to rationalize it. Don't be defensive.

10. Have a trusted colleague assess your daily interactions with people.

11. Review your notes from several years worth of feedback sessions and performance reviews with your bosses. What trends do you see? What no longer appears as a weakness? This is valuable data for you.

12. In determining areas you want to improve, don't take on too big of a list. If you do, you will likely fail in at least some of the items. Limit yourself to 1-5 behaviors or practices that you feel need to be improved.

13. As you design a plan of attack on your targeted areas, consider your current workload, your supervisor's agenda and expectations for you, time demands away from your job, and other relevant factors. Considering these will bring a healthy dose of reality to your plan and minimize discouragement later.

14. Sharing your personal development intentions with a trusted colleague, coach, mentor, or friend will prove to be a big advantage and incentive to stick to your goal. They will encourage you and provide support.

15. Once you begin your self-development plan or efforts, take it as seriously as you would any other part of your regular job responsibilities. Stick with it.

16. Consider raising the bar for your strengths. Push your-self to new and higher levels of performance. Your strengths are your greatest asset.

17. One of the biggest career stoppers is being unable to adapt to differences and changes. Assess how adapt-able you are.

18. Be careful of being overly ambitious. Those who are may be more inclined to "manage up" far more than "down" or "sideways." All three directions should be balanced.

19. As you plan and prepare to rise in your organization, pick your battles wisely and carefully. Keep your emo-tions under control.

20. Nothing can ever beat out genuine, irrefutable hard work. It will be noted by others and will label you as solid. It will overshadow gamesmanship, manipula-tion, and self-promotion.

21. Develop a demonstrated track record of helping oth-ers. This will elevate you in their eyes and come back to you several times over.

22. Try to appreciate how other people feel about issues.

23. Review your personal habits, mannerisms, idiosyn-crasies, and group behaviors.

24. Consider analyzing your current job requirements. What aspects do you enjoy the most and why? Leveraging these areas can bring success.

25. Ask yourself how you handle rejection of your ideas or suggestions.

26. Measure how much emotional support you provide to others.

27. Sense when a colleague needs to talk. When that happens, listen with limited talking.

28. Does your temper or a short fuse hinder your effectiveness?

29. Can you listen to contrary viewpoints?

30. Understand that different situations call for different skills and approaches.

31. Recognize that what got you to your current position may not be the skills, knowledge, and abilities that will take you to the next level. New capabilities will be required.

32. Identify and seek out assignments that will stretch you.

33. Identify blind spots and develop ways to counter them.

34. Identify a mentor or coach to help you grow.

35. Smile more. Remember, it takes many more muscles to smile than to frown.

36. Act as if what you do is a pleasure. It will send powerful signals to everyone.

37. Your humility, balanced with solid confidence, will be admired by your people.

38. Cultivate patience. It is the only way you can deal with all that life throws at you.

References

Emotional Intelligence: Why It Can Matter More Than I.Q.; Daniel Goleman, Bantam, 1994.

StrengthsFinder 2.0: A New and Upgraded Edition of the Online Test from Gallup's Now, Discover Your Strengths; Tom Rath, Gallup Press, 2007.

The Etiquette Advantage In Business: Personal Skills For Professional Success; Peggy Post, Peter Post, Harper Collins, 1999.

Attitude: The Choice Is Yours; Michele Mattyanna, AMI How-To Series, American Media Publishing, 1996.

Why CEOs Fail; David Dotlich, Peter Cairo, Jossey-Bass, 2003.

People Skills; Robert Botton, Touchstone Books, 1986.

True Professionalism: The Courage to Care About Your People, Your Clients, and Your Career; David H. Maister, Simon & Schuster Adult Publishing Group, 2000.

What Got You Here Won't Get You There; Marshall Goldsmith, Profile Books, 2008.

Talent is Overrated: What Really Separates World-class Performers from Everybody Else; Geoff Colvin, Penguin Books, 2008.

The Five Temptations of a CEO; Patrick Lencioni, Jossey-Boss, 1998.

Now, Discover Your Strengths; Marcus Buckingham, Donald Clifton, Free Press, 2001.

The Rules of Work; Richard Templar, Prentice Hall Business, 2003.

Self-assessment

 Using the scale provided, rate yourself on the following leadership behaviors.

Poor   Excellent

1   2   3   4   5   6   7

_____ I dedicate time each week for personal development.

_____ I utilize my peers and/or colleagues as coaches and feedback providers.

_____ I attend professional development and networking events.

_____ I strive to apply new tools or learning in my day-to-day work.

_____ I balance my home and work life.

_____ I maintain interests/hobbies outside of work.

_____ I have good relationships inside and outside of work.

Comments:

Action Planning Notes

 What three things in this section will help you be a better leader?

1.

2.

3.

What would change if you started or continued doing these three things?

How can you implement these changes?

Dimension 15: Team Building

"Coming together is a beginning. Keeping together is progress. Working together is success."

— Henry Ford

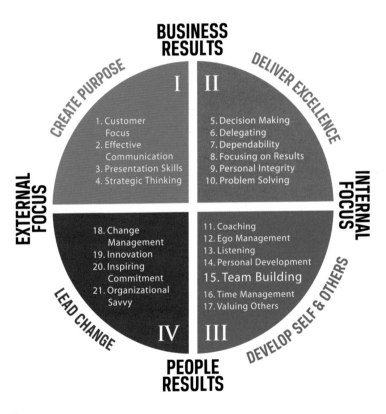

BUSINESS RESULTS

CREATE PURPOSE

DELIVER EXCELLENCE

EXTERNAL FOCUS

INTERNAL FOCUS

I
1. Customer Focus
2. Effective Communication
3. Presentation Skills
4. Strategic Thinking

II
5. Decision Making
6. Delegating
7. Dependability
8. Focusing on Results
9. Personal Integrity
10. Problem Solving

IV
18. Change Management
19. Innovation
20. Inspiring Commitment
21. Organizational Savvy

III
11. Coaching
12. Ego Management
13. Listening
14. Personal Development
15. Team Building
16. Time Management
17. Valuing Others

LEAD CHANGE

DEVELOP SELF & OTHERS

PEOPLE RESULTS

Overview

Maximum performance can only be achieved through others. A well-orchestrated team can produce far more than any group of individuals. Your role as the team leader is best summarized by the following essential activities: organizing the players, planning, mentoring, acknowledging performance and contribution, addressing problems and conflict, clarifying the big picture, communicating clearly, and a never ending amount of *listening*.

To help you be more effective as a team builder, consider the following tips:

Tips

1. Include your people in setting goals, solving problems, and making decisions that affect them. It will give them a sense of inclusion and ownership. It will also build their capacity and help them feel valued.

2. Make sure your team is always in the communication loop. This will ensure that they feel like a part of the team. It will also prepare them to deal with changes and issues as they surface.

3. Your team members deserve your support when problems and challenges occur.

4. Effective conflict resolution among team members is crucial for keeping the team united. Healthy and appropriate disagreement is desirable when debating ideas; personal conflict between team members is not.

5. The single most effective behavior by a leader in building a team is to be honest, ethical, and trusted by the team.

6. A leader must *first* be sure he or she clearly communicates the vision, mission, purpose, and focus to the team. *Second*, the leader must make sure there is ongoing communication with the team.

7. Openness of ideas and input among the team is essential. Healthy, honest debate is a hallmark of a productive team, but once the decision is made, the debate ends and everyone needs to support the decision.

8. The major share of activity and resources must be focused on achieving the team's or organization's primary goals.

9. The leader needs to champion the team to upper management. The team needs to see, feel, and believe that their leader goes to bat for them.

10. Some teams are "self-directed" in that they determine their own purpose, direction, and approach without an official leader. The team members share leadership. Under certain circumstances, this arrangement can be very productive and advantageous—but training is needed to get them started.

11. A very successful team leader is seen as a facilitator for the team rather than a boss.

12. A classic model of team development involves four stages of a team's growth: 1) forming, 2) storming, 3) norming, and 4) performing. These terms will help you track the progress of your team's evolution.

13. Tom Peters (author of *In Search of Excellence*) says effective team leaders are "barrier breakers." They do all they can to clear the road so the team can keep moving ahead.

14. Team leaders need to give feedback to team members: positive in public, negative done privately—separating the person from the behavior.

15. Identify team norms in advance. These will define such internal matters as handling conflict, celebrating suc-

cesses, conducting meetings, making decisions, and prioritizing time and resources. These are separate from performance goals and objectives given the team by upper management.

16. Leverage strengths across the team, especially to minimize weaknesses.

17. Create a shared, mutually understood, and accepted goal designed primarily by the team.

18. Bring a group of diverse individuals together. Varied backgrounds are much better than homogeneity.

19. Over the course of a project, conduct honest assessments of the team's effectiveness and cohesion.

20. Periodically assign a "fool" (devil's advocate) to take opposing views. (This is a temporary role and must not become permanent.)

21. Be open to the team's feedback and advice to you, as their leader.

22. Tune into your people's favorite radio station: "WIIFM" (*What's In It For Me*). Keep this in mind as you lead them. They are always interested in their own welfare.

23. Individual communication to your people must not be limited to correcting poor performance. Positive and encouraging feedback is also essential.

24. Greet and acknowledge people often. Their performance will reflect your attention.

25. A healthy, professional, and uplifting sense of humor brings a refreshing influence to your team. Avoid sarcasm and put-down humor.

26. The critical components of effective relationships are directly influenced by:

- the frequency of communication with them
- your sincere concern for their well-being
- your consistency in how you treat them

27. Overall characteristics of a successful team:

- The team's purpose and objectives are clear.
- Roles and responsibilities are understood.
- All members are committed and actively participating.
- Members listen to each other.
- People are comfortable in disagreeing, doing it in a healthy manner.
- The team treats each other with mutual respect.
- An atmosphere of fun exists.
- Members recognize and appreciate each other.
- SMEs (Subject Matter Experts) are identified and utilized.
- Conflict is natural on issues, not people.
- Information should flow freely in all directions.

28. Key Attributes of a team leader and members:

- Trusting
- Respectful
- Open
- Collaborative
- Supportive
- Follows through
- Encouraging
- Participative
- Non-threatening

References

The Wisdom of Teams; J.R. Katzenbach, Harper Business, 1993.

Team of Rivals: The Political Genius of Abraham Lincoln; Doris Kearns Goodwin, Simon & Schuster, 2005.

The One Minute Manager Builds Performance Teams; Ken Blanchard, Don Carew, Eunice Parisi-Carew, Morrow & Company, 1990.

Making 2+2=5: 22 Action Steps Leaders Take to Boost Productivity; John H. Zenger, Irwin, 1996.

Creating the High Performance Team; Steve Buchholz, Thomas Roth, John Wiley & Sons, 1987.

Team Players and Teamwork: The New Competitive Business Strategy; Glenn Parker, Jossey-Boss, 1990.

The Five Dysfunctions of a Team: A Leadership Fable; Patrick M. Lencioni, Jossey-Bass, 2002.

The New Why Teams Don't Work: What Goes Wrong and How to Make It Right; Harvey Robbins, Michael Finley, Berrett-Koehler Publishers, 2000.

The Carrot Principle; Adrian Gostick, Chester Elton, Free Press, 2009.

The 17 Essential Qualities of a Team Player; John C. Maxwell, Maxwell Motivational Books, 2002.

Strengths-Based Leadership; Tom Rath, Barry Conchie, Gallup Press, 2008.

Self-assessment

 Using the scale provided, rate yourself on the following leadership behaviors.

Poor   Excellent

1   2   3   4   5   6   7

_____ I create an environment for open and honest communication.

_____ I trust my people.

_____ My people trust each other.

_____ My people trust me.

_____ I leverage the strengths of each team member.

_____ I recognize the efforts and accomplishments of each team member.

Action Planning Notes

 What three things in this section will help you be a better leader?

1.

2.

3.

What would change if you started or continued doing these three things?

How can you implement these changes?

Dimension 16: Time Management

"Work expands so as to fill the time available for its completion."

— Prof. C. N. Parkinson

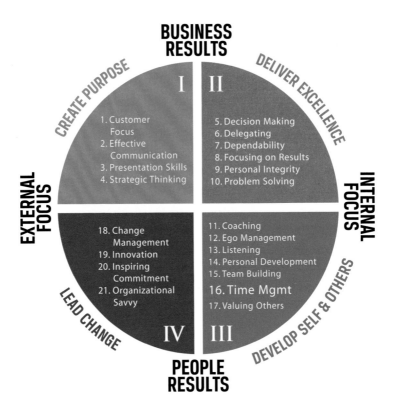

BUSINESS RESULTS

CREATE PURPOSE

DELIVER EXCELLENCE

EXTERNAL FOCUS

INTERNAL FOCUS

I

1. Customer Focus
2. Effective Communication
3. Presentation Skills
4. Strategic Thinking

II

5. Decision Making
6. Delegating
7. Dependability
8. Focusing on Results
9. Personal Integrity
10. Problem Solving

IV

18. Change Management
19. Innovation
20. Inspiring Commitment
21. Organizational Savvy

III

11. Coaching
12. Ego Management
13. Listening
14. Personal Development
15. Team Building
16. Time Mgmt
17. Valuing Others

LEAD CHANGE

DEVELOP SELF & OTHERS

PEOPLE RESULTS

Overview

Each person, no matter their status, education, potential, or talents only has twenty-four hours in the day. How those twenty-four hours are used determines the essence of their lives, what they accomplish, and who they become. It is easy to fritter away hours with nothing to show for it. Personal motivation and discipline, along with teachable techniques are essential to using your time wisely. Your need to take time for family, sustain relationships, let yourself exhale, meet your supervisor's deadlines, and dozens of other life demands all fill up your limited time allotment. This is not easy. It can be difficult balancing all that life seems to deal out.

To help you be more effective in managing your time, consider the following tips:

Tips

1. Focus on high leverage actions and activities. Determine priorities each week that will lead to accomplishing your major goals.

2. One of the hardest things to learn appears to be the most simple. It is merely this: Do the most important things first. Unimportant things can eat up your day.

3. Your mind is limited in its scope, so only concentrate on a few actions or projects at a time. Otherwise you will dilute your effectiveness on all of your activities.

4. Identify and select those aspects of your job that have the biggest payoff. These areas deserve the major portion of your time, energy, and resources. Treat them as sacred—otherwise they will be eroded by lesser things.

5. Recognize windows of opportunity. Take advantage of them before they close. Make every minute count. No, you don't have to be a workaholic, but when you have limited time, use it wisely and well. Avoid time robbers.

6. Don't be a slave to email or texting. Set aside certain times to do them. They can be marvelous tools when used effectively. They can also enslave you.

7. Make deadlines for yourself and keep them. Only shift them when you absolutely have to.

8. Spend time (such as driving, commuting, or airplane travel) to think of ways your team or organization can be more effective—ways they can improve performance.

9. List the things that are debilitating to your effectiveness. What can you do about them? Yes, some are beyond your control, but others can be addressed productively by making changes in your own behavior and habits.

10. Analyze the way you run meetings. Can they be shorter? Do you use an agenda? Are items brought up that could be handled off-line with just one person? Ask your people for their input and ideas for overall improvements.

11. "Open door" polices have many advantages, but you have every right to "closed door" time each day so you can get through your must-do items.

12. Parkinson's Law says that "work expands to fill the time available for its completion." So, be aware of this typical behavioral tendency when establishing deadlines for yourself and others.

13. Recognize the value of small bits of time. These are gifts to help you through your major activities. Think of all the "ten-minute chunks" that you have in a day, especially at airports, in taxis, or waiting for others. Use them to chip away at priority big projects. You'll be surprised at your progress over time.

14. By making a plan for each day, you will establish a basic guide for your day. Determine high-payoff items versus low-payoff items—the 80/20 rule. Even though you will experience events that will likely interrupt your plan, you will accomplish more and you will feel in greater control of your life.

15. Learn to say "no" to unimportant or nonessential activities. You must be the ultimate judge of how you spend your time. If your objectives are already defined in your mind, then your judgment of what is essential and what is not will be much easier.

16. Record due dates. Prioritize. Delegate whenever possible. Match your strategic priorities with your calendar time. Minimize non-core activities. Separate your activities into four categories: mission critical, important, nice to do, and not central.

17. Organize your work area so others can locate items when you are gone.

18. Write down and prioritize "to do" items, so you won't forget.

19. Handle each piece of paper only once. Apply the same strategy to email.

20. Have your people represent you at meetings when possible. It will give them an opportunity for growth.

21. Schedule personal, private catch-up time. Many executives set aside two hours early each morning.

22. Before leaving work each day, briefly plan for tomorrow.

23. Follow through with commitments. (This will give you a very positive reputation in being dependable.)

24. Be punctual. Show up at meetings on time. When in

charge, start meetings on time.

25. Monitor how you spend your time for any given week. Analyze and learn from it.

26. Return phone calls when you are most likely to get through. Text when brief messages will suffice.

27. Be sensitive to the need for a "work/life" balance.

28. Don't take other people's "monkeys" or responsibilities. This often happens without the individual realizing it.

29. If you consistently spend excessive time looking for things, your system needs overhauling.

30. Ask yourself, "Am I available to my people for some portion of each day?" (Would they agree?) Be sensitive to others' time.

31. At the start of each day, know what your most important tasks are.

32. Does the Internet or other digital devices excessively sidetrack you? If so, re-think their use to your advantage.

33. If you travel often, have a set of duplicate items to save you time—such as power chargers and cords. The same applies to toiletries.

34. Be sure you aren't guided solely by what you like and dislike.

35. Identify what part of the day you are most effective and schedule mission-critical items then.

36. Determine and analyze when and why you procrastinate.

37. Ask for suggestions on how to improve from colleagues and family members.

References

The Procrastinator's Handbook: Mastering the Art of Doing It Now; Rita Emmett, Walker & Company, 2000.

The 25 Best Time Management Tools and Techniques: How to Get More Done Without Driving Yourself Crazy; Pamela Dodd, Doug Sundheim, Peak Performance Press, 2005.

Time Management from the Inside Out: The Foolproof System for Taking Control of Your Schedule—and Your Life; Julie Morgenstern, Holt Paperbacks, 2004.

How to Run a Successful Meeting in Half the Time; by Milo Frank, Simon & Schuster, 1990.

Right on Time!: The Complete Guide for Time-pressured Managers; Lester R.Bittel, McGraw-Hill, 1991.

Getting Things Done: The Art of Stress-Free Productivity; David Allen, Viking Penguin, 2001.

The First 90 Days: Critical Success Strategies for New Leaders at All Levels; Michael Watkins, Harvard Business School Press, 2003.

Self-assessment

 Using the scale provided, rate yourself on the following leadership behaviors.

Poor   Excellent

1   2   3   4   5   6   7

_____ I regularly prioritize my daily tasks and responsibilities.

_____ I effectively manage short- and long-term objectives and commitments.

_____ I know how to identify and stop doing non-core activities.

_____ I clearly delegate activities to others.

_____ I control my schedule instead of my schedule controlling me.

_____ I know what to say "no" to.

_____ I am prepared for meetings.

_____ I use electronic devices to my advantage.

Comments:

Action Planning Notes

 What three things in this section will help you be a better leader?

1.

2.

3.

What would change if you started or continued doing these three things?

How can you implement these changes?

Dimension 17: Valuing Others

"Kind words can be short and easy to speak, but their echoes are truly endless."

— Mother Teresa

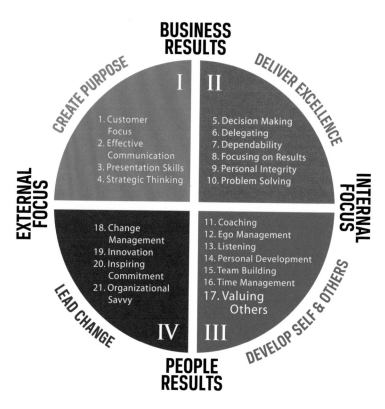

BUSINESS RESULTS

CREATE PURPOSE

I
1. Customer Focus
2. Effective Communication
3. Presentation Skills
4. Strategic Thinking

DELIVER EXCELLENCE

II
5. Decision Making
6. Delegating
7. Dependability
8. Focusing on Results
9. Personal Integrity
10. Problem Solving

EXTERNAL FOCUS

INTERNAL FOCUS

IV
18. Change Management
19. Innovation
20. Inspiring Commitment
21. Organizational Savvy

III
11. Coaching
12. Ego Management
13. Listening
14. Personal Development
15. Team Building
16. Time Management
17. Valuing Others

LEAD CHANGE

DEVELOP SELF & OTHERS

PEOPLE RESULTS

Overview

It seems that all human beings are born with a sign around their neck that reads, "I want to feel like I make a difference!" Each of us has a need to feel valued, and that we make a difference in the world—in our sphere of influence. You can do many things to fuel this desirable attitude of positive self-worth in your people. These are behaviors and practices that can be taught and learned. You can substantially influence their lives.

To help you be more effective in valuing others, consider the following tips:

Tips

1. Speak out when others are not being valued or recognized for their contribution. Encourage others to share their thoughts and suggestions. Help them to be heard. Facilitate their views being considered and taken into account.

2. Give feedback respectfully and helpfully so others can realize growth opportunities and pinpoint ways to improve.

3. Be alert for developmental programs and courses, and then share these with others.

4. Ask yourself, "Who have I not recognized or connected with this past week that I should have?"

5. Share credit often.

6. Celebrate successes (no budget required). There are many "no expense" ways to have mini celebrations.

7. Treat others with respect. Never demean others.

8. Do not interrupt others or finish their sentences.

9. Include others in decisions. Ask them for their opinions.

10. Build rapport with associates by asking questions that show genuine interest in them. Where do they live?

How long have they worked here? What is their favorite vacation? What do they enjoy doing after work?

11. Go to their workstation or cubicle to get to know them. Note any personal photos and mementos that they have on display. Build conversations around those topics.

12. Respect their time.

13. Be careful not to hurt or diminish others without realizing it through careless comments, nonverbal cues, or thoughtless behaviors that leave others feeling inferior, silly, or unqualified.

14. Be compassionate and understanding.

15. Be fair and reasonable.

16. Be consistent in your treatment of everyone. When you are consistent, no one feels unfairly treated, picked on, or negatively singled out.

17. Mentor others officially or unofficially. Help them learn the ropes, paths of opportunities, and steps to take for growth and recognition.

18. Learn more about those behaviors and practices that build and reinforce a genuine feeling of value in others. Work to make these practices a part of your toolbox

19. *Before* making a decision, look at the ramifications it will likely have on others. Step into their shoes. How will the end result impact them? Are there consequences that are unintended and harmful to others that have not been considered?

20. Remember how you felt when you were younger in the organization. This will remind you of the way others may feel right now. Consider their feelings, concerns, and attitudes as you make decisions.

21. The need for including others in communication loops cannot be overstated. People feel unappreciated, ignored, and unimportant when they are not part of the communication loop.

22. Make every effort to let them know what is happening. Keep others current on plans, directions, decisions, and concerns. Take advantage of company/corporate newsletters, publications, bulletin boards, announcements, emails, etc. As a result, they will feel valued. They will feel a sense of ownership. They will work harder because their commitment is higher and stronger.

23. Become familiar with various personality assessments (such as the *Myers-Briggs Type Indicator*) to give you a greater understanding and appreciation for the many varieties of people you work with and how your style/type relates to them.

24. Be careful not to make assumptions and generalizations about people. These are often unfair and unkind. They also make you appear shallow and short-sighted. People deserve the right to prove themselves based on their own merits, efforts, and accomplishments. This also reflects the value they have for themselves.

25. Value the contribution others make in areas outside of their work. Recognize their involvement in civic affairs, art, theater, music, athletics, church, school, youth groups, and volunteer work. Learn what they are involved in and acknowledge the time and talents that they volunteer.

26. Recognize that people tend to do what they believe is

in their best interest.

27. Publicly acknowledge your team and/or key individual performances. When praising, be specific about where and how people have excelled.

28. Be motivated to help others, not yourself. Seek to make them look good. As a result, their consequent commitment to you will be much higher.

29. Get into the habit of complimenting others—sincerely and genuinely point out what they do well.

30. Personal hand written notes expressing specific appreciation for "extra mile" efforts are very effective. They mean more than an email.

31. Build objectives that assess and recognize positive team and individual performance into regular performance appraisals. Teach supervisors how important this is in valuing others.

32. The easiest way to let others know you care is to call them by name. Learn what they prefer to be called and use it (nicknames, initials, shortened names, etc.). When using email, spell their names correctly.

33. It's amazing what can get accomplished if you don't care who gets the credit. Share credit.

34. Try your best to be available when others need you.

35. Develop formal awards programs that receive wide attention. Always be specific when making the presentations.

36. When giving feedback, be specific, timely, and sincere.

37. When giving corrective feedback, which can be received as negative, separate the person from the act. Condemn the act—reinforce the person.

References

1001 Ways to Reward Employees; Bob Nelson, Workman Publishing, 1994.

Encouraging the Heart: A Leader's Guide to Rewarding and Recognizing Others; James M. Kouzes, Barry Posner, Jossey-Bass, 1999.

The Human Value of the Enterprise: Valuing People as Assets: Monitoring, Measuring, Managing; Andrew Mayo, Nicholas Brealey Publishing, 2001.

The Human Equation: Building Profits by Putting People First; Jeffrey Pfeffer, Harvard Business School Press, 1998.

Quest for Balance: The Human Element in Performance Management Systems; André A. de Waal, John Wiley & Sons, 2002.

Love and Profit: The Art of Caring Leadership; James A. Autry, Harper Paperbacks, 1992.

The Carrot Principle; Adrian Gostick, Chester Elton, Free Press, 2009.

Common Sense Management: Quick Wisdom for Good Managers; Roger Fulton, Ten Speed Press, 2009.

Self-assessment

 Using the scale provided, rate yourself on the following leadership behaviors.

Poor   Excellent

1   2   3   4   5   6   7

_____ I share credit with others.

_____ I provide clear, specific, and actionable feedback.

_____ I try to abide by the 4:1 ratio (four positive comments to one constructive comment).

_____ I am available to support my people.

_____ I listen to my people's concerns and hopes.

_____ I remove obstacles so my people can be successful.

_____ I do not demean others through sarcasm, put-downs, or side comments.

Comments:

Action Planning Notes

 What three things in this section will help you be a better leader?

1.

2.

3.

What would change if you started or continued doing these three things?

How can you implement these changes?

Dimension 18: Change Management

"It is not the strongest species that survive, nor the most intelligent, but the ones who are most responsive to change."

— Charles Darwin

Overview

Nothing is as constant as change. Organizations do not survive if they do not respond and adapt favorably to the world around them. Yet, many employees resist change. You have seen what happens to organizations that do not embrace new technologies, respond to new marketplace demands, develop new business opportunities, and understand evolving employee attitudes and needs. Your obligation to your business is to learn the essentials of change, how to communicate change, what the resistors are, and the vital role you play in making it all happen. You need to be a champion of change. Look for opportunities to improve every aspect of the business.

To help you be more effective in managing change, consider these tips:

Tips
Purpose and Plan

1. When planning any type of change, always include and involve those affected by it.

2. Make sure when embarking on a change initiative that the goal or end result is clear to all involved.

3. Be attentive to and learn from change efforts outside your organization. Analyze what has succeeded and what has failed as others have tried similar efforts.

4. Look at the type of change you are proposing. Is it gradual or sudden? Is there urgency? Why? These answers will help you determine your change communication strategy.

5. Compare your proposal to other efforts you have been involved in. What is the difference? What went well and what aspects of it went poorly? How can you learn from this?

6. All change has pros and cons. Face your proposed ini-

tiative with your eyes open. Beware of blind spots.

7. Decide where you are now and where you want to be. This gap will determine and define your initial change purpose and strategy.

8. Identify and define all resources (people, technology, capital, time) that will be required.

9. What will the initial and lasting impact of the change be?

10. Be able to state the business case in 2-3 sentences. Frame the case for change for all levels of stakeholders.

11. Develop a project and communication plan.

12. Play the fool (devil's advocate) to critically test your ideas.

Sponsor and Stakeholders

13. Build alliances that will support the change initiative. Carefully study the resistance you are likely to encounter. Explore why—what are the reasons? Anticipate these and prepare contingencies to mitigate them.

14. Recognize your own strengths and how they can support your change effort. Areas you are deficient in will require change partners who have talents in those areas.

15. Analyze your own resistance to previous change initiatives. Others may have similar feelings.

16. Change efforts that succeed must clearly demonstrate direct benefits to employees and customers. If one of these is ignored, lasting change will not likely occur.

17. Ask employees and customers for their opinions before, during, and after the change. Seek their advice and counsel.

18. Never underestimate or overlook competing agendas.

19. Make certain that all goals, responsibilities, assignments, and schedules are CLEAR to everyone involved.

20. Ensure a specific sponsor exists for the change.

21. In most cases, as uncomfortable as it may be, political fences must be mended.

22. You must be absolutely convinced about what you believe needs to be changed. Prove this to yourself over time before you begin the change itself.

23. Identify, develop, and maintain strategic partnerships.

24. Test the climate with a mentor or trusted associate. Encourage the mentor to give you an honest reality check.

25. Remember change will require campaigning, lobbying, bargaining, caucusing, negotiating, collaborating, etc.

26. Remember, buy-in from those affected is absolutely essential.

27. Consider the cultural impact of the change.

28. The single most important action you can take to get people to adhere to a new policy, procedure, or request is to tell them how they will benefit—what's in it for them.

Implement

29. How will you address impacted processes and the continuity of work?

30. Develop well thought-out transition plans bridging the old with the new.

31. Once the change is underway, seek out early successes and recognize them. Also, hold small discussion

groups to hear concerns, impediments, and frustrations related to the change effort.

32. Develop a team of "believers"—the able and willing.

33. Align processes with HR systems. Do the HR systems need to change first?

34. Remember that the change effort will take much longer than you think.

35. Assign a dedicated person or team to manage the change.

36. Make sure the people leading the change have time and authority to do it.

37. Identify clear measures of success for the project and for the business impact. Report on these regularly during the change effort.

38. Conduct surveys, focus groups, etc. to determine challenges and successes.

References

Leading Change; John P. Kotter, Harvard Business School Press, 1996.

First, Break All the Rules: What the World's Greatest Managers Do Differently; Marcus Buckingham, Curt Coffman, Simon & Schuster, 1999.

Only the Paranoid Survive: How to Exploit the Crisis Points that Challenge Every Company and Career; Spencer Johnson, Putnam, 1998.

Rules for Revolutionaries; Guy Kawasaki, Harper Business, 1999.

Who Moved My Cheese?: An Amazing Way to Deal with

Change in Your Work and in Your Life; Spencer Johnson, Putnam, 1998.

The Change Masters; Rosabeth Moss Kanter, Simon & Schuster, 1983.

Our Iceberg Is Melting: Changing and Succeeding Under Any Conditions; John Kotter, St. Martin's Press, 2006.

Influencer: The Power to Change Anything; Kerry Patterson, Joseph Grenny, David Maxfield, McGraw Hill, 2008.

Managing Transition: Making the Most of Change; 2nd Ed., William Bridges, Perseus Books, 2003.

Champions of Change: How CEOs and their Companies are Mastering the Skills of Radical Change; David Nadler, Jossey Boss, 1998.

The Change Masters: Innovation for Productivity in the American Corporation; Rosabeth Moss Kanter, Simon & Schuster, 1983.

The First 90 Days: Critical Success Strategies for New Leaders at All Levels; Michael Watkins, Harvard Business School Press, 2003.

The Heart of Change; John P. Kotter, Dan Cohen, Harvard Business School Press, 2002.

Deep Change: Discovering the Leader Within; Robert E. Quinn, John Wiley & Sons, 1996.

The Art and Practice of Leadership Coaching; Howard Morgan, Phil Hawkins, Marshall Goldsmith, John Wiley & Sons, 2005.

Self-assessment

 Using the scale provided, rate yourself on the following leadership behaviors.

Poor   Excellent

1   2   3   4   5   6   7

_____ I am a clear champion for change efforts.

_____ I clearly communicate the business case for change to all stakeholders.

_____ I use my authority to help employees remove roadblocks, which impede employees' performance and progress.

_____ I have credibility in the organization.

_____ I build alliances to make desired changes stick.

_____ I include those affected by the change in the change process.

Comments:

Action Planning Notes

What three things in this section will help you be a better leader?

1.

2.

3.

Change Management

What would change if you started or continued doing these three things?

How can you implement these changes?

Dimension 19: Innovation

"Nothing is so embarrassing as watching someone do something that you said couldn't be done."

— Sam Ewing

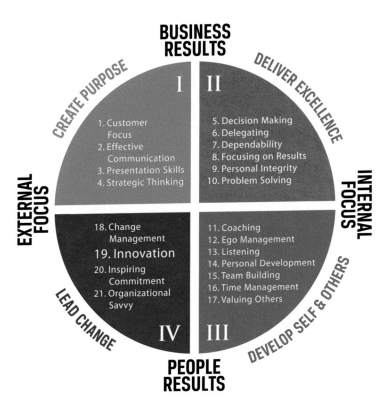

Overview

A leader's challenge is to build a culture that fosters creativity and innovation. A positive sign of such a culture is seeing your people originate new ideas and sharing

them with you. This requires a sense of belonging, owner-ship, and accountability among your people so that they want to contribute far more than the minimum, and con-sequently grow and improve every aspect of the business. Ideas sometimes come from the least expected sources. Be alert for them and encourage off-the-wall thinking from your team. It will add a sense of fun to the workday. Create a positive environment that supports the value of good ideas and how they make a difference. The future demands an environment of innovation.

To help you be more effective in handling and manag-ing all aspects of innovation, consider the following tips:

Tips

1. Argue other viewpoints. Examine the possible. Analyze the impossible. Change your hypothesis. Alter the scene. Distort the "facts" as you know them. Make your ideas into reality—what would change? View fail-ure as success. Act like there is no risk. How will these actions open up new ideas?

2. Beware of idea killers:
   - We've always done it this way.
   - But I didn't think of it.
   - The boss wouldn't like it.
   - We could never afford it.
   - We tried it before and it didn't work.
   - It won't work.
   - That's ridiculous.
   - Are you crazy?

3. Look for relationships among seemingly unrelated ideas and concepts. Often the obvious obscures the

more meaningful insights.

4. Avoid the tendency to make snap judgments of an idea.

5. Share the concept with someone from another discipline. They will take a fresh, objective viewpoint that you probably have not considered.

6. See what those outside of your organization have done with similar issues or opportunities. What can you learn from their experience, progress, or limitations?

7. Instead of asking "*why?*" try asking "*why not?*"

8. Be careful of premature censoring of ideas or solutions. Analyze the criteria you are using. It may be too narrow or limiting.

9. Group-generated thinking usually produces greater quality of input. This is especially true if the group is comfortable with each other. Laughter and fun will unlock greater creativity and generate many ideas. Out of the dozens of ideas they may come up with, two or three could become your million dollar answer.

10. Look at information, journals, online sources, books, and resources that you usually don't read in order to obtain a fresh perspective.

11. Ask "*what if . . .?*" and see what follows.

12. Try listening to music. It might open new mental avenues.

13. Acknowledge that people have higher creative periods during certain parts of the day than others. Mornings are often better than afternoons for idea generation. Take advantage of peak times.

14. Drawing or illustrating a problem will often stimulate mental processes more than just words. Use a large board and write out your thoughts. Keep your ideas

visible for others to see.

15. How you view a situation or problem usually determines how you approach it. This can lead to mental ruts. Try to alter your view and notice how your approach will also adjust accordingly.

16. Pursue outside resources to shed additional light on the subject. Consider nearby university faculty, industry representatives, trade shows, conferences, lectures, publications, or retired colleagues.

17. Avoid "reinventing the wheel." Build on the work of others in the past or recently. Learn from their work. Leverage it. Develop it. Try new patterns and develop them. Create your new designs and solutions as you springboard off the thinking of others.

18. Be an example to your team in demonstrating "out of the box" thinking. Lead by example in suggesting a variety of options to addressing problems. This needs to include all types of alternative solutions.

19. One of the biggest drawbacks to innovative thinking is believing that you are not creative. Change your view of yourself, because you are much more creative than you think.

20. Manage your ego. Carefully consider the inputs and suggestions of others.

21. Ask how a 9-year old would approach it.

22. Remember 6 minutes of healthy, uninhibited brainstorming can often produce 48 inputs. Then after 20 minutes of hard evaluation, these 48 can be reduced to 2-3 solid ideas.

23. Blend partial answers from divergent ideas.

References

Corporate Creativity: How Innovations and Improvement Actually Happen; Alan Robinson, Sam Stern, Berrett-Koehler Publishers, 1987.

A Whack on the Side of the Head; Roger von Oech, Warner, 1983.

The Creativity Infusion; R.D. Gamache, Robert Kuhn, Bellinger, 1989.

The Ten Faces of Innovation: IDEO's Strategies for Beating the Devil's Advocate and Driving Creativity Throughout Your Organization; Tom Kelley, Jonathan Littman, Doubleday Publishing, 2005.

Innovation: The Five Disciplines for Creating What Customers Want; Curtis R. Carlson, William W. Wilmot, Random House Inc, 2006.

The Innovator's Dilemma: The Revolutionary Book that Will Change the Way You Do Business; Clayton M. Christensen, Collins Business, 2003.

Talent is Overrated: What Really Separates World-class Performers from Everybody Else; Geoff Colvin, Penguin Books, 2008.

Self-assessment

 Using the scale provided, rate yourself on the following leadership behaviors.

Poor   Excellent

1   2   3   4   5   6   7

_____ I recognize that I don't have a monopoly on new ideas.

_____ I welcome new ideas or approaches.

_____ I encourage brainstorming without critique.

_____ I am willing to take appropriate risks.

_____ I am up-to-date on best practices and industry trends.

_____ I am never satisfied with the status quo and try to look for new ways to make it better.

Comments:

Action Planning Notes

 What three things in this section will help you be a better leader?

1.

2.

3.

Innovation

———•———

What would change if you started or continued doing these three things?

How can you implement these changes?

Dimension 20: Inspiring Commitment

"It is not fair to ask of others what you are not willing to do yourself."

— Eleanor Roosevelt

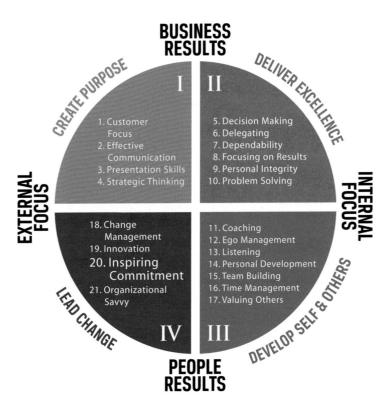

BUSINESS RESULTS

CREATE PURPOSE

DELIVER EXCELLENCE

I
1. Customer Focus
2. Effective Communication
3. Presentation Skills
4. Strategic Thinking

II
5. Decision Making
6. Delegating
7. Dependability
8. Focusing on Results
9. Personal Integrity
10. Problem Solving

EXTERNAL FOCUS

INTERNAL FOCUS

IV
18. Change Management
19. Innovation
20. Inspiring Commitment
21. Organizational Savvy

III
11. Coaching
12. Ego Management
13. Listening
14. Personal Development
15. Team Building
16. Time Management
17. Valuing Others

LEAD CHANGE

DEVELOP SELF & OTHERS

PEOPLE RESULTS

Overview

Machines tend to be predictable and fairly constant. When one malfunctions, a good reliable manual or instruction book will usually contain the answer. But people are an entirely different breed of complexity and unpredictability. They come with no reliable manual. A new part, changed fuse, or re-built hard drive does not do the job. There may be any number of causes for changes in performance or attitude. Your objective as a leader is to stay on top of each of your players, knowing what makes them tick, their hot buttons, concerns, and strengths. Leaders must create an atmosphere where people are engaged and committed. This requires many components and behaviors from the leader to reap the solid and pro-ductive performance that you expect.

To improve your effectiveness in inspiring commitment among your associates, consider the following tips:

Tips

1. People perform better when they know what is expect-ed of them. Make certain that performance standards are clearly defined, communicated, and documented so there is no doubt what the expectations are.

2. Discuss expectations openly with employees and en-courage questions and additional information they have which will affect their buy-in and their performance.

3. Be the champion of your group or team to upper management. Share their achievements and perform-ance with others in a positive way to bring light and support to your people. This will clearly demonstrate your pride in your people!

4. Clarify all related rewards, compensation, and incen-tives that will influence performance in writing.

5. Never ask others to do what you are not willing to do yourself.

6. Seek ways to expand their authority, respectability, and span of control as they progress and grow. This will give them the sense that you care about them and want to help them move ahead.

7. Ask your people how they are doing, and how you can help.

8. Recognize their performance. Share credit freely and openly.

9. Seek opinions and welcome suggestions from your people in areas that they know well.

10. Know your associates well enough that you recognize aspects of their job or of related jobs that may provide them greater satisfaction. When possible, direct them to those opportunities.

11. Develop team spirit and camaraderie within the workgroup. Strong team bonds among workers lead to high levels of loyalty, performance, and commitment.

12. Be aware of what rewards and recognitions are meaningful to them. Provide these when appropriate. (Don't rely on what worked for you in previous organizations. Attitudes will vary from company to company and from person to person.)

13. Make sure they know you will support them, defend them, explain for them, and go to bat for them. They need to know they can count on you as their advocate to upper management. Once this is clear, you will be amazed by what they are willing to do.

14. Not everyone is happy in every situation. There comes a time when some individuals will find greater satisfaction in other work areas or assignments. Accept this as OK. When it happens, help them find more suitable work in other organizations. You will both be

happier if you do.

15. Build on the belief that every person's work and function is important. Avoid favorites. Every one of them is vital to the overall purpose.

16. If you ask an employee to do work that you used to do, be careful that you do not watch too closely. If you do, they will naturally begin to doubt your trust in their ability. Also, they will likely not do the job the way you did, and this is acceptable if the final product meets agreed upon standards.

17. Treat everyone consistently. Be fair. They notice favoritism as well as someone being targeted and picked on.

18. Do all you can to create a high performance culture and environment. Employees' work attitude usually is a reflection of their work environment.

19. Genuine, active listening to your employees will do more to gain their commitment than any other single behavior.

20. Share the "why" behind decisions whenever possible. Knowing the why will give them a greater understanding and sense of purpose.

21. Celebrate successes.

22. Let people do their job. Don't micromanage.

23. Clarify the "what" (purpose) and leave the "how" (methods) up to the employees. It will let them feel ownership.

24. Make certain your actions communicate your solid support of your people.

25. When people sense that you have their best interests at heart, they respond more favorably to your requests.

26. Express your requests to others in ways that appeal to them—not to you.

27. Create a vision, communicate it clearly and rally your team around it. Be able to explain your vision in just a few sentences. Be consistent about sharing and describing the same vision. This helps create alignment with the vision.

28. Recognize employees from their perspective—what's important to them.

References

1001 Ways to Energize Employees; Bob Nelson, Workman, 1997.

The Disney Way: Harnessing the Management Secrets of Disney in Your Company; Bill Capodagli, Lynn Jackson, McGraw-Hill, 1999.

GUNG HO: Turn On the People in Any Organization; Ken Blanchard, Sheldon Bowles, Morrow & Company, 1998.

Real Change Leaders: How You Can Create Growth and High Performance at Your Company; Jon R. Katzenbach, Times Business (Random House), 1997.

Who: The A Method For Hiring; Geoff Smart, Randy Street, Ballantine Books, 2008.

Good to Great: Why Some Companies Make the Leap . . . and Others Don't; Jim Collins, Collins Business, 2001.

Master Motivator: Secrets of Inspiring Leadership; Mark Victor Hansen, Joe Batten, Jim Rohn, Fall River Press, 2005.

Learned Optimism: How to Change Your Mind and Your Life; Martin E.P. Seligman, First Vintage Books, 2006.

The Carrot Principle; Adrian Gostick, Chester Elton, Free Press, 2009.

Strengths-Based Leadership; Tom Rath, Barry Conchie, Gallup Press, 2008.

Common Sense Management: Quick Wisdom for Good Managers; Roger Fulton, Ten Speed Press, 2009.

Self-assessment

 Using the scale provided, rate yourself on the following leadership behaviors.

Poor   Excellent

1   2   3   4   5   6   7

_____ I promote each person's strengths.

_____ I support and defend my people.

_____ I share the "why" behind a decision or request.

_____ I recognize the efforts and accomplishments of others.

_____ I clearly describe a meaningful future vision.

Comments:

Action Planning Notes

 What three things in this section will help you be a better leader?

1.

2.

3.

What would change if you started or continued doing these three things?

How can you implement these changes?

Dimension 21: Organizational Savvy

"Organizational Savvy is having the necessary information and internal knowledge of people, systems, cultures, and sub-systems to GET THINGS DONE."

— Anonymous

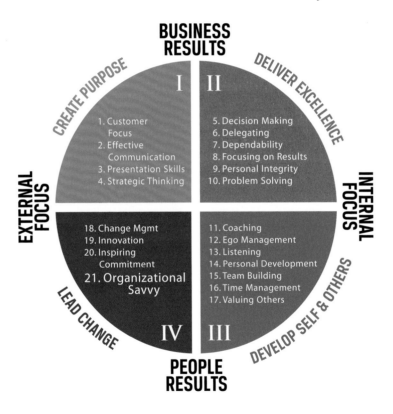

Overview

Organizational Savvy is also known as organizational agility, or the ability to know how to get things done

197

within the business. To have this you must know several vital aspects about the company, the business, or your department. Primarily you know key people—the shakers and movers! You know who to call, who can do what, who is willing, who knows who, who has the authority, who can make it happen, who knows the history, who knows the unwritten rules, who can break the logjam, who knows the way around the policies, who owes you a favor, and who likes a good challenge. These relationships are the key to getting what needs to be done DONE! This requires knowledge of both the formal channels and the informal channels, the origin and thinking behind "policies, practices, and procedures," and a thorough understanding of the culture—past, present, and future.

To help you be more effective in developing organizational savvy, consider the following tips:

Tips

1. A handy rule of thumb is the word *SEEK*. To have "Organizational Savvy," you must *SEEK* the following:
   - **S**upport—who can provide it for you
   - **E**quipment—what you'll need and how to get it
   - **E**xperience—who knows the right people and their respective "hot buttons"
   - **K**nowledge—who knows how things really work, and how things get done

2. Learn how you are viewed in the company from the perspective of your boss or other senior colleagues and modify your behavior accordingly.

3. When you anticipate resistance to an idea you're preparing to present to a key group, consider pre-sell-

ing it to members of the group one at a time (lobby-ing). Also know the "unofficial" organization chart. This will require learning who has "real" power.

4. Know the organizational chart. Know boundaries and cross-overs of functional responsibilities.

5. Learn internal "partnerships" and unofficial strong relationships between key individuals so you can leverage and capitalize on them.

6. Establish a network of professionals within your organization who know the business, the company, the products, the services, the customers, and the markets—especially those that affect your own sphere of concern and interest, and may benefit and help you. Rotate through the list regularly for a lunch or brief visit to learn their perspective and opinions. Get to know them. Have them know you.

7. Be knowledgeable about the unofficial and official key players in the organization, their personalities, philosophies, behaviors, attitudes, track records, and agendas.

8. Be aware of your major competitors and their methods—external AND internal.

9. Learn who knows who outside of work. What are the relationships?

10. When significant events happen in your company, learn how they happened, who drove it, why it was accomplished, and special or unusual circumstances that accompanied it.

11. Know names, faces, and history of your organization's major customers and suppliers.

12. Pay attention to the grapevine. It is a potent source of information.

13. Recognize that titles are not always indicative of actual power players. Learn the difference. Stay tuned to the genuine catalysts and action people.

14. Consider characteristics and attitudes of key decision makers so you can develop your team's strategies when you need senior management's support. Learn their stand on various issues (pros, cons, neutral) to help ensure the success of your plan.

15. Do consistently good work and *subtlety* make it visible to key decision makers.

16. Network with others outside of your organization.

17. Learn the history of critical parts of the company and culture that affect your group—what has worked, what hasn't worked, and why.

18. Sort through data and pick out important items.

19. Influence where you have no authority by building your personal credibility.

20. Stay current on best practices and industry trends.

21. Recognize that informal and formal organizations are not the same.

22. Identify the opinion leaders and the networkers in the organizations.

23. Be forward thinking.

24. Pay close attention to what is happening in the work environment: from a 35,000-foot point of view and a 5,000-foot view.

References

The Balancing Act: Mastering the Competitive Demands of Leadership; Kerry Patterson, Joseph Grenny, Ron McMillan, Al Switzler, Thomson Executive Press, 1996.

The Greatest Management Principle in the World: The Success Secret for Anyone Who Works for a Living; Michael LeBoeuf, Putnam, 1985.

What They Don't Teach You at the Harvard Business School: Notes From a Street-Smart Executive; Mark H. McCormack, Bantam, 1984.

Influence Without Authority; Allan C. Cohen, D.L. Bradford, John Wiley & Sons, 1990.

Survival In the Corporate Fishbowl; John P. Fernandez, Lexington, 1987.

Power and Influence: Beyond Formal Authority; John P. Kotter, Free Press, 1986.

Control Your Destiny or Someone Else Will; Noel M. Tichy, Stratford Sherman, HarperCollins Publishers, 2005.

Champions of Change: How CEOs and their Companies are Mastering the Skills of Radical Change; David Nadler, Jossey-Boss, 1998.

Warren Buffet's Management Secrets: Power Tools for Personal and Business Success; Mary Buffet, David Clark, Simon & Schuster, 2009.

The Rules of Work; Richard Templar, Prentice Hall Business, 2003.

Self-assessment

 Using the scale provided, rate yourself on the following leadership behaviors.

Poor   Excellent

1   2   3   4   5   6   7

_____ I have credibility in the organization.

_____ I use my authority to help employees remove road-blocks, which impede the employees' performance and progress.

_____ I help employees see the "Big Picture" and how their responsibilities and performance affect it.

_____ I have a well developed internal network.

_____ I have a well developed external network.

_____ I am aware of the unofficial organization chart and who the movers and shakers really are.

Comments:

Action Planning Notes

 What three things in this section will help you be a better leader?

1.

2.

3.

What would change if you started or continued doing these three things?

How can you implement these changes?

Section III

Included in this last section are assessments, leadership exercises, reflection questions, and action plan forms to turn your intent into measurable improvements.

Chapter Four
Assessments

There are three assessments in this chapter:

1. *LEAD NOW! Model* Self-assessment
2. *LEAD NOW! Leadership Dimensions* Assessment
3. Most Desired Leadership Behaviors in an Ideal Leader

1. LEAD NOW! Model Self-assessment

Self-assessment
Consider your personal leadership development in each of the four quadrants of the *LEAD NOW! Model*. Evaluate your skill in each quadrant using the following scale. Descriptions for each quadrant are on the following page.

LEAD NOW! MODEL

LEAD NOW! Model Description

Quadrant I: Create Purpose
(Externally Focused Business Results)

A leader is responsible for defining the group's vision and strategy. *Creating Purpose* identifies what the organization stands for, what it is going to do, and how it is positioned in the marketplace. This involves studying the competition, thoroughly knowing the customer, analyzing industry trends, setting strategy, and communicating effectively to others.

Quadrant II: Deliver Excellence

(Internally Focused Business Results)

A leader is responsible for delivering operational excellence—translating the strategy into day-to-day execution for the organization. This involves clear decision making, the ability to build consistent and measurable processes, continuous improvement, and behaving with integrity.

Quadrant III: Develop Self & Others

(Internally Focused People Results)

A leader must value learning for him/herself and for others. This involves seeking personal improvement opportunities, building and managing team dynamics, honing technical expertise, managing one's time, coaching and developing others, and managing one's ego.

Quadrant IV: Lead Change

(Externally Focused People Results)

A leader is responsible for creating and championing change efforts that will benefit the organization. This involves influencing key decision makers, sponsoring change projects, empowering stakeholders, encouraging innovation, managing resistance, and making change stick.

2. LEAD NOW! Leadership Dimensions Assessment

Self-assessment

Consider your personal leadership development in each of the Dimensions of the *LEAD NOW! Model*. Rate your understanding and skill in each dimension using the following scale:

Poor   Excellent

1   2   3   4   5   6   7

Comments:

LEAD NOW! MODEL
21 Leadership Dimensions

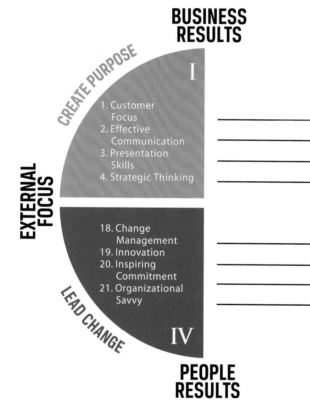

BUSINESS RESULTS

CREATE PURPOSE

I

1. Customer Focus
2. Effective Communication
3. Presentation Skills
4. Strategic Thinking

EXTERNAL FOCUS

18. Change Management
19. Innovation
20. Inspiring Commitment
21. Organizational Savvy

LEAD CHANGE

IV

PEOPLE RESULTS

LEAD NOW! MODEL
21 Leadership Dimensions

BUSINESS RESULTS

DELIVER EXCELLENCE

II

5. Decision Making
6. Delegating
7. Dependability
8. Focusing on Results
9. Personal Integrity
10. Problem Solving

INTERNAL FOCUS

11. Coaching
12. Ego Management
13. Listening
14. Personal Development
15. Team Building
16. Time Management
17. Valuing Others

III

DEVELOP SELF & OTHERS

PEOPLE RESULTS

What trends do you see? Which Dimensions in the model stand out? Your highest-rated Dimensions represent strengths you should leverage, while your lowest-rated are areas for improvement.

3. Most Desired Leadership Behaviors in an Ideal Leader

The following is a list of the top ten behaviors of an ideal leader. It was compiled from over 8,000 responses to our 360-degree leadership assessment that we administered to Fortune 500 and government agency executives, managers, and employees. Each participant was asked to rank the top behaviors of an "ideal leader" (one they would like to work for), out of 78 leadership behaviors.

These are the highest-rated behaviors that executives, managers, and employees believe an ideal leader should do. Note that they are listed in order from highest to lowest, so the first trait is the most desired.

1. Lives, manages, and works with integrity. (Quad II)

2. Follows through on actions, promises, and assignments. (Quad II)

3. Has the technical expertise to do his/her job. (Quad III)

4. Is fair, open, and professional in dealing with employees. (Quad I)

5. Has credibility in the organization. (Quad IV)

6. Is loyal to his/her people. (Quad III)

7. Treats others with dignity. (Quad III)

8. Works to solve problems rather than avoiding them, making excuses, or blaming others. (Quad II)

9. Tries to see that excellent performance by his or her people is recognized. (Quad III, IV)

10. Is focused on the needs of the customer. (Quad I)

Self-assessment

Consider how well you perform each of these "Most Desired" leadership behaviors and answer the following questions.

1. Which behaviors are you currently doing well? How can you leverage these strengths?

2. Which behaviors represent areas that you could change and improve?

3. Why do you feel the need to focus on these behaviors?

4. How will you make this a priority?

Chapter Five
Leadership Exercises

There are five Leadership Exercises in this chapter:

1. My Personal Philosophy of Leadership
2. Ideal Leader
3. Ideal Peer/Team Member
4. Ideal Direct Report
5. Team Charter

These exercises will provide you with additional tools to use with your team in a variety of leadership situations. They may apply to your current assignment or to a future team you are going to lead.

The first one is particularly useful when you are leading a new group. First, complete it by yourself through honest introspection, and then share it with your new team. As you do so, tell your team members that it describes your style and philosophy, and is not intended for them to copy you. You are merely saving them time in learning what you expect and how you operate. Too often a new group will spin their wheels for too many months trying to figure out what makes the new boss tick. By learning more about you early on, they will be able to respond to your requests sooner and more effectively because they have a better understanding of you.

The next three exercises are designed to help the team open up to each other by learning what everyone prefers in behaviors and practices of the "ideal" leader, peers or team members, and direct reports. This is advantageous in helping the team learn what behaviors are regarded high vs. low priority to each member of the team. This process will open up vital discussion for the team in learning more about itself.

The final exercise is very effective in aligning a team around a common purpose. It is a tool that promotes healthy and needed discussion in defining the direction of the team.

1. My Personal Philosophy of Leadership

In this exercise, you should identify what matters most to you as a leader by the four parts of your Personal Philosophy of Leadership: I) My Style and Operating Principles, II) My Values, III) My Preferences, and IV) My Pet Peeves.

This exercise will help you organize and optimize your abilities to work and lead effectively. And, perhaps more importantly, when shared with your people, it will greatly improve their ability to work effectively with you. This is helpful for a new leader or a leader with a new team.

I. My Style and Operating Principles:

How would you define your leadership style? How do you establish goals and objectives for your team? How do you reach decisions and implement them? How do you manage budgets and schedules? How do you direct the efforts of your team members and direct reports? How do you organize your workload and your office space? How do you handle and learn from mistakes, successes, new challenges, etc.? How do you delegate and handle collaborative work?

II. My Values:

What values drive your decisions and actions as an individual and as a leader? What values matter most to you in others? These might include honesty, trust, loyalty, religious views, self-discipline, work ethic, etc.

III. My Preferences:

If you could prioritize everything in your work environment to meet your preferences, what would you do? What day of the week/time of the day would you hold meetings? When would you read and respond to email? How do you prefer to communicate with others (face-to-face, email, phone, etc.) and how frequently? When do you want to be available for your people (i.e., "open office hours")? When would you rather not be disturbed? How do you prefer to provide feedback and coaching? What is your preferred office attire? How would you ideally balance your work and home life? How do you prefer to direct group discussion, brainstorming, and problem-solving? How do you prefer to handle office politics?

IV: My Pet Peeves:

What behaviors and actions get under your skin? Is there a time of day when you are the least effective? Do you struggle in working with chatty people? Does it bother you when people are late? Does it bother you when people send multiple emails without giving you a chance to respond? Does it bother you when people are uptight or stiff, or, on the other hand, when people are too informal? Do you hate it when someone interrupts your workflow? What are the idiosyncratic behaviors that drive you crazy?

I. My Style And Operating Principles

II. My Values

III. My Personal Preferences

IV. My Pet Peeves

2. Ideal Leader

This exercise is designed to help you identify the skills, behaviors, and characteristics that you value most in a boss.

Think back through all the bosses you've had. If you were able to magically create the "ideal boss," one you would love reporting to, what attributes and behaviors would you include? Be as specific as possible. Each person in the team can complete this and compare responses.

-

-

-

-

-

-

-

-

3. Ideal Peer/Team Member

This exercise is designed to help you identify the skills, behaviors, and characteristics that you value most in a peer or team member.

Think back through all the peers or teammates you've had. If you were able to magically create the "ideal peer or team member," one you would love working with, what attributes and behaviors would you include? Be as specific as possible. Each person in the team can complete this and compare responses.

-
-
-
-
-
-
-
-

4. Ideal Direct Report

This exercise is designed to help you identify the skills, behaviors, and characteristics that you value most in a direct report.

Think back through all the direct reports you've had. If you were able to magically create the "ideal direct report," one you would love having report to you, what attributes and behaviors would you include? Be as specific as possible. Each person in the team can complete this and compare responses.

-

-

-

-

-

-

-

-

5. Team Charter

The Team Charter helps align a team around a common purpose—what the team's purpose is and how to achieve it. This exercise is best completed together as a team. It is great for a new leader, a new team, or at the start of a project. The team can periodically reference and review this charter to ensure unity and alignment with agreed upon vision.

Complete this team charter as a team as a means of aligning the team.

Our team's purpose (1-3 sentences):

Our top five stakeholders and customers:

1.

2.

3.

4.

5.

LEAD NOW!

Performance results expected from our team:
- Cost:
- Quality:
- Speed:
- Service:
- Quantity:

Our team norms:

-

-

-

-

-

-

-

-

Source: Preston Pond, Center for Organizational Design

Reflection Questions

What Leadership Dimensions are helpful to you?

What tips will help you develop?

What resources will help you develop?

What are other thoughts and ideas that will help you develop?

Action Planning

What would be different if you used these tips and resources?

Chapter Six

Action Planning

Bridging knowledge and practice

Your action plans will be more meaningful and effective if you draw from your assessments and the tips included in relevant sections. So before writing up your action plans, review all your assessments and the sections of *LEAD NOW!* that apply to the areas you want to improve.

Action Plans

In order to help you operationalize what you learned in *LEAD NOW!*, we have provided Action Plan worksheets.

Keep the following information in mind as you make your own action plans.

Effective goal statements

Setting appropriate goals is often difficult. As you formulate your goal statements for each action plan, ask yourself these questions, which represent the essential elements of an appropriate goal:

- Is it realistic (challenging, but not too difficult)?
- Is it challenging enough (will it really push you to improve)?
- Is it measurable (do you know if you are progressing)?
- Is it dated (when will it be achieved)?

One last question: who will you share it with? Accountability is a key to achieving your goal.

Sample Action Plans

We have provided two sample action plans on the following pages. These demonstrate effective goal statements and focus areas.

Action Plan - Sample

Name: Pat Ling   **Today's Date:** 5.15.11

Behavior or practice to change: Quality of team meetings

Goal statement: By August 2011, achieve increased participation from all team members and improved follow-up.

Reason for Changing: So that all team members are on board and supportive of decisions

Benefits that will come from changing: Better participation and team decisions

Focus Area	Actions	Support	Timeframe
Planning	Have written agenda for each person	Assign to a team member (rotate each week)	Permanently
My behavior	Do not voice my own opinion until the end of the discussion	Write "DON'T SAY IT" on post-it note on my notebook	All 3rd quarter
Get them involved	Ask, "What do you think?" of everyone	Ask William to remind me if I forget	Each weekly meeting
Follow-up actions	Ask them to restate their part in assignments	Have a review in the last 5 min. of the meeting	Each weekly meeting

Potential Barriers:
Too many topics to cover on agenda.

Mitigation:
Adjust the agenda or arrange to conduct follow-up afterward.

Action Plan - Sample

Name: Chris Jackson   **Today's Date:** 4.2.11

Behavior or practice to change: Time management

Goal statement: I will make my selected time management skills a consistent part of my daily/weekly routine by 9.2.11

Reason for Changing: I keep getting behind in my work.

Benefits that will come from changing: Tasks will be done on time, boss will be happier, I won't be as frustrated.

Focus Area	Actions	Support	Timeframe
Email	Don't leave work until I've answered email	Put post-it note on my computer	Trial period for 8 weeks
Begin projects sooner	Use "lulls" to work on small pieces of large tasks	Project team partner	All of this quarter
Planning	Spend 30 min. each Sunday night planning my week	My spouse	Next 2 months
Other time management skills	Review list of "tips" in LEAD NOW!	Leave book by bedside	Sunday nights

Potential Barriers:
I get overwhelmed again and get discouraged.

Mitigation:
Allow myself to start over with above steps. I'm only human.

Action Plan

Name: Today's Date:

Behavior or practice to change:

Goal statement:

Reason for Changing:

Benefits that will come from changing:

Focus Area	Actions	Support	Timeframe

Potential Barriers: Mitigation:

Action Plan

Name: Today's Date:

Behavior or practice to change:

Goal statement:

Reason for Changing:

Benefits that will come from changing:

Focus Area	Actions	Support	Timeframe

Potential Barriers: Mitigation:

Action Plan

Name: Today's Date:

Behavior or practice to change:

Goal statement:

Reason for Changing:

Benefits that will come from changing:

Focus Area	Actions	Support	Timeframe

Potential Barriers: Mitigation:

Action Plan

Name: Today's Date:

Behavior or practice to change:

Goal statement:

Reason for Changing:

Benefits that will come from changing:

Focus Area	Actions	Support	Timeframe

Potential Barriers: Mitigation:

Action Plan

Name: Today's Date:

Behavior or practice to change:

Goal statement:

Reason for Changing:

Benefits that will come from changing:

Focus Area	Actions	Support	Timeframe

Potential Barriers: Mitigation:

Notes

Notes

Notes

Notes

Author

John Parker Stewart

John is an internationally recognized executive coach, leadership and organization consultant, sought-after speaker, national award winning trainer, orals coach for government contractors, and author. Over the past 35 years, he has coached and trained tens of thousands of leaders worldwide. He specializes in team performance, executive development, change management, and leadership training. He managed executive and leadership development for 86,000 employees at Lockheed Corp where he designed and taught the Lockheed Executive Institutes for

13 years. He started Stewart Systems, Inc. in 1980, where he has researched, consulted, taught, and coached thousands of leaders—CEOs, presidents, executives, and managers—including all levels of management at Kennedy Space Center over an eight year period.

After attending the University of Colorado, John received his bachelor's degree from Brigham Young University. He completed his master's degree in Organizational Communication and wrote his thesis in London, with additional graduate work and teaching at Michigan State University. He performed more graduate studies under management guru Peter Drucker at Claremont Graduate School. John was selected "National Trainer of the Year" by the American Society for Training and Development for two consecutive years.

He has researched organizations and worked with corporations worldwide. His client list includes NASA, Lockheed Martin, Citibank, Toshiba, Xerox, Chevron, Raytheon, CSL-Hong Kong, GM, Shell Oil-Malaysia, Kaiser Permanente, Telstra-Australia, US Air Force, US Dept of Energy, Kennedy Space Center, Boeing, IBM, Rockwell, BAE Systems, TVA, Duke Energy, Northrop Grumman, and many other government agencies and commercial firms.

John resides in Lake Oswego, Oregon.

Visit his website: www.johnparkerstewart.com

Author

Daniel J. Stewart

Daniel J. Stewart specializes in leading large-scale organization development and change management efforts. Over the past ten years, he has been an internal and external OD practitioner delivering leadership and team development, organization design, coaching, strategic planning, and process improvement for companies like Kohl's Department Stores, JetBlue Airways, Avaya Telecommunications, Lockheed Martin, and VC start-ups.

Daniel holds a master's degree in Organizational Communication and Development from the University of Colorado at Boulder and a Bachelor's degree in International Relations from Brigham Young University. He is published in *Executive Excellence*, *Practicing OD*, *Proposal Management (APMP) Journal*, and HR.com.

Daniel resides in Milwaukee, Wisconsin